Sailing Three Oceans

2000
Best Wishes,
Herb & Doris Smith

Sailing Three Oceans

Building and Sailing Schooner *Appledore*

by
Herbert and Doris Smith

A Peter Randall Book

Published by
Down East Books

For Tom, Lisa and Susan

Edited and Designed by Peter E. Randall

ISBN: 0 - 89272 - 261 - 4

A Peter Randall Book

Published by   Down East Books
Camden, ME

Library of Congress Cataloging-in-Publication Data
Smith, Herbert, 1941-
        Sailing Three Oceans : building and sailing schooner Appledore /
by Herbert and Doris Smith
            p.   cm.
        "A Peter Randall book."
        ISBN 0-89272-261-4
        I. Appledore (Ship) 2. Voyages around the world--1981-
I. Smith, Doris, 1951- . II. Title
G440.A62S55 1988
910.4'1--dc 19   88-18988
                                                  CIP

9 8 7 6 5 4 3 2

Tom in the rigging entering Durban.

What would life be without difficulties and problems.
There is a terrific exaltation in overcoming difficulties:
victory, triumph, elation, jubilance. Unless you pit
yourself against something that is very hard and struggle,
you are never going to have exhilaration. Hold onto your
dreams. If your dreams are broken you are like a winged
bird that cannot fly.

Norman Vincent Peale

Doris and the children making friends at Port Eden.

Herb drilling for keel bolt, Appledore III.

6

Preface

Many of the people my wife, Doris, and I meet in the course of our travels are eager to know how we chose our lifestyle. Did we come from seafaring families? How did we secure enough money to build a sailing vessel? How did we find the time to sail it around the world? What's it really like sailing the oceans? This book has been written to answer such frequently asked questions.

Schooner *Appledore* began as a daydream when I was growing up in Portsmouth, New Hampshire. There I often passed the restored homes of legendary sea captains such as John Paul Jones, and I yearned to share in the romance of owning and captaining a traditional wooden sailing vessel. As a daydreamer sailing on the estuaries of the Piscataqua River, I began setting goals, and I later found out people can achieve their goals without conscious effort. In fact, I believe that a daydreamer is secretly guided and motivated by an unconscious creative force.

After high school, I joined the United States Coast Guard and soon found myself on the deck of the ice-breaker *Eastwind*, bound for Antarctica. *Eastwind* introduced me to an ocean that so many people never see: the great expanse of blue water stretching from horizon to horizon, alternately offering peace and tempest, according to the dictates of Nature. En route to Antarctica, the ship took me to exotic islands in the South Pacific: Tahiti, Pitcairn, Fiji, Samoa, Australia, and New Zealand. These ports in turn infected me with an incurable love of adventure — with the islands of the South Pacific always my focal point and the great oceans always the route.

I have written most of this book from the skipper's point of view, but included extracts from Doris's log to give a different perspective to some of the events. During our several voyages, we have had many good crew members, and they certainly are part of the overall story, but we decided to focus here on our own family and on the adventures shared by the four of us.

(above) Appledore I, *(below)* Appledore II, *(opposite)* Appledore III, *off Tahiti.*

(above) North Country winter, 20 below zero. Appledore III *under construction in building at left. (below) White oak pieces of a schooner ready for assembly.*

(above) Plunking Appledore III. *(below) Crooked Reach, Strait of Magellan.*

Playa Parta, with Strait of Magellan in the background.

Off Cape Froward.

Peel Inlet, Patagonia Channel.

(left) Sheep rancher, Punta Arenas. (below) Puerto Montt shop.

Seaman, Puerto Montt.

(above) Juan Fernandez Island. (below) Easter Island.

Appledore *off Pitcairn Island.*

Tom and Lisa on a dark sand beach, Tahiti.

Contents

(above) Herb on assignment filming whales, 1972. (below) Herb and Lisa, Appledore III, *1985.*

A Career Change

There is no feeling like that of being on board a boat propelled by wind alone. It is a quiet, peaceful feeling. The only sounds on board are the hiss of sea water passing by the hull, the squeaking of leather in the rigging, and the occasional rustle of a sail. There is the feeling of freedom from the concerns of daily life. It's just you and the elements. The breeze blowing past your ears whispers of ports half a world away.

It was 1972, and with my lack of knowledge of boatbuilding, I had to be a bit crazy or, at best, a born optimist to think I could build a 48-foot schooner in my backyard. However, I had just returned from Hollywood and several years in the motion-picture industry, where fantasy and impossible dreams are part of the fabric of many people's lives. I was also anxious to return to Portsmouth, New Hampshire, because Doris Plante was on her summer recess from the University of Maine.

After returning to Portsmouth, I obtained permission from Mrs. Walter Ross to erect a plastic building in her backyard, ideally situated on the edge of Portsmouth's back channel. I had spent many days in that yard as a boy, learning the ins and outs of the lobster-fishing business from her late husband. On retiring from the trade he had sold me all of his equipment, which I used most summers. Mrs. Ross, now alone at 74, seemed to welcome the renewed activity just above the tide line.

In the following months, Bud McIntosh, a boatbuilder and designer from nearby Dover, became not only my mentor but also a close friend. A Dartmouth graduate, Bud is a natural-born teacher, and I was not the only pupil he was leading by the hand through the boatbuilding process. I never failed to notice the twinkle in his eyes as he entered a boatshop and saw the haggard novice enveloped in total frustration. Bud always acted as though what you were doing was ridiculously simple, and, at the time he was giving instructions, it did in fact seem simple. But

(above) Bud McIntosh working on Appledore I. *(below) Doris in the hull of* Appledore I.

panic would set in after he said, "Now just do as I did and I'll be back in a few days to help you on the next step." "But what about the other side? Doesn't the angle change?" His sly grin would always return. "Oh, you can figure it out. There's nothing to it."

Probably the best lesson Bud taught me was how to get the job done. A builder who works on his own boat has a tendency to be too fussy, adding months, even years, to the time needed to complete a project. As Bud would say, "There are those who fuss and accomplish nothing and then there are those who just get the job done." I can't remember how many times I heard the comment, "It's perfectly all right."

I had worked alone for a few months, reaching the stage of having the boat framed, when I became impatient and decided romance be damned. Time and money never last as long as anyone anticipates. I had to get more work done on the boat. I borrowed $11,000 from an understanding bank after being turned down by six others. Then I hired George Guptill and Forrest Stillings to help plank. Bud McIntosh came each week to supervise. I had to get the boat completed enough to launch and then go back to work for Walt Disney Productions. I was running out of money.

With mortgage payments due, I took an assignment with Disney that put me on the icebreaker *Southwind*, headed for the Arctic. My job was to take photographs of icebergs and wildlife to be used for the backdrops in *Islands on Top of the World*. After the long hours I had worked to build *Appledore*, it was a welcome break. I had sailed several times aboard icebreakers headed for the Antarctic, and even though I found Greenland and Iceland intriguing on this expedition, I missed the Pacific islands that were part of the Antarctic voyages. Yet, after a couple of months, *Appledore* and Doris began to haunt my dreams. I was overjoyed when fall arrived and I was able to return to Portsmouth.

Even though *Appledore* had been launched before I left, I had plenty of work still to do. In fact, I had ahead of me just as many hours as I had worked before. Now it was the interior, the masts and spars, and the rigging.

It was not long after beginning work on the interior that I realized I never wanted to be a finish carpenter. Time seemed to fly, yet little ever showed in the way of accomplishment. After watching me rip out a set of shelves three times in that many days, Doris insisted that I should remember Bud's advice about not being too fussy and to get the job done. She reminded me that although she was willing to move on board and even live in uncomfortable conditions for a while, even a saint would eventually run out of patience.

With April came the cleansing rains that washed away the snow and brought warm air to set ones blood astir. On a calm day, we towed *Appledore* across the river to the salt docks, where a crane hoisted her

Maiden voyage of Appledore I, *Doris at the helm.*

masts into place. Work on the interior came to a halt, and I moved up on deck to finish rigging her. By early May, I was satisfied that she was ready for her maiden voyage.

On May 8, 1974, I telephoned the keepers of the Memorial Bridge, a draw that spans the Piscataqua River between Maine and New Hampshire. I told them we would be heading downriver at 10 a.m., the time of slack water and the only time we would be able to navigate this river of strong currents. Since we had no engine and the bridge was less than a quarter-mile away, I was concerned that they would not hear my signals and not raise the middle span in time.

At 9:45 a.m., I instructed Doris, who was nervously pacing up and down the dock, on what lines to let go and what lines I would be asking her to sheet. Even though she was a lobsterman's daughter, she had never sailed before, and this was all a mystery to her.

Friends watched as I called to Doris to let go the bow line and sheet in the jib. As the wind filled the jib, the bow began to fall away from the dock and we were off on a tack across the river. As we approached the opposite shore, I waited anxiously to see how well *Appledore* would come about, but as I pushed the tiller hard over, I knew I had nothing to fear. She came about easily, responding beautifully. We were now ready to make our approach to the bridge. Having watched us outfit *Appledore* for the previous six months, the bridgekeepers were waiting for us to pass beneath, and gave us a special siren signal of congratulations and farewell.

I was impressed with the way *Appledore* cut effortlessly through the water, patterns of white foam peeling away from her hull. She was a thing of beauty. Fred White in his lobsterboat motored alongside and timed our progress: "Seven-and-a-half knots," he yelled over to us. Not bad for the little wind we had, I thought.

Once out of the mouth of the Piscataqua, we sailed back and forth, using two tankers anchored offshore as an obstacle course. For the early part of the day, we simply relaxed, enjoying the feel of the boat.

At dusk, we arrived in Gosport Harbor at the Isles of Shoals. We anchored in front of Appledore Island in 60 feet of water, letting out 200 feet of line. After a pleasant dinner, we watched the sun set over the mainland. Many years earlier, from this same anchorage, I had seen a lobsterman's small daughter waving from the doorway of her father's house on Appledore Island. Coincidentally—and perhaps fatefully—it was Doris. Little did she or I realize that we would meet again, that she would become my wife and that we would sail around the world together in a ship named for that island.

Anyone who has ever had sailing fever knows how addicting and all-consuming it is. For five glorious days we did nothing but sail. It was a craving that could not be satisfied. I did not feel the cold or the rain. Hunger eluded me. It was as if I could never get enough miles under the hull.. At the same time, Doris's practical nature took over, and she reminded me that we had to prepare for a charter that was only a few weeks away.

Our first week-long charter was in Rockland, Maine, 120 miles to the northeast. We left Portsmouth on July 1, a light southwest breeze moving us down the coast. The first night, we anchored off Wood Island near Old Orchard Beach, where we spent a few days visiting with relatives and taking them out on *Appledore*. On July 4, we got underway again, bound for Boothbay Harbor.

The wind was blowing from the southeast at 8 knots most of the morning, and we averaged about 4 knots. By mid-afternoon, however, the wind died and the fog rolled in. After sitting on a sea of glass for almost two hours with all sails set, I suddenly noticed that the sky had a different look to it.

Instead of being the usual dismal gray, it began to take on a dark purplish hue. Visibility was no more than a few hundred feet, so it was difficult to see what was approaching. No sooner had I asked Doris to pass up my raingear than all hell broke loose. Eighty knots of wind struck, heeling us over 75 degrees. I was thankful that *Appledore* was a new boat and that her sails and rigging were at their best. Fortunately, the portlights along the cabin sides were closed, since they now were under water. After about a minute, we came up suddenly, the rigging and sails still intact. Then we were knocked down again from the other side.

Doris was down below and viewed all this from a different perspective:

> I had just given Herb his raingear and had gone up forward to get another set when I felt the boat begin to lay over on its side. At first, I paid no attention, since I had finally gained enough confidence in the boat to think she would never roll over. However, the roll did not stop, and books, sheets, and blankets began falling out of their shelves and onto the cabin sole in front of me. I had recently seen the movie *Poseidon Adventure* in which an ocean liner is turned over by a huge wave. The people in the ship were trapped inside. What flashed through my mind was the scene in which the piano is suspended from the floor. Before I could imagine the piano falling, I was on my way out. If I was going to drown, I was not going to be trapped, as those people in *Poseidon* were, below decks. Smitty, our cat, had the same idea. She and I scrambled for the after hatch, struggling to see who was

going to get up the ladder first. Once on deck, I was shocked by what I saw. The rain and wind whipped my body, and within seconds I was drenched to the bone. Although my teeth chattered, it was due more to fright than cold. Herb had promised me *Appledore* would not roll over, but as I huddled in the corner of the cockpit watching the masts hover above the frothy surface of the water, I didn't believe a word of it. To make matters worse, Herb had gone up forward to see if he could release the jibsheet. We may have been down only a minute, but it seemed like hours. We righted suddenly and I was just breathing a sigh of relief and thanking God for sparing us when the wind hit us again. This time, I finally began to regain my composure. After all, we had withstood one knockdown already. I even got the nerve to get up and try to rescue our spare main boom, which was floating away. It was a good thing we had two knockdowns. It is like falling off a horse. If you get right back on, you defeat your fear. After the first knockdown I was determined to quit sailing and conceded my mother was right that the sea is no place for a woman. After the second knockdown, it became a challenge.

There were many reports of tornadoes that day. Once the storm passed, the fog lifted and the wind shifted to the east, but it was dead against us, so we spent several more hours tacking into Boothbay Harbor. We dropped the anchor at 11:00 p.m. and crawled into our bunks, exhausted.

On July 7, we arrived in Rockland in time to pick up our passengers from Albany, New York. That probably was the most-appreciated charter we have ever done. Perhaps it had a lot to do with our own enthusiasm. Being on our first extended charter, we were as excited as they were. We spent five days and nights sailing the islands of Penobscot Bay, stopping at Deer Isle, Camp Island, Isle au Haut, and Vinalhaven. One of the men claimed it was the greatest vacation he had ever had, and they kept in touch with us for several years.

Our second charter, on August 2, was with a family of four from Bronxville, New York. This was our last week-long charter that summer—a poor showing for the season. For several weeks, we stayed at anchor in Boothbay Harbor. At that time, there was still room to anchor in the inner harbor, and we were well protected from the swells. The town was as quaint and picturesque as any we had seen. After talking to the people who were chartering the schooner *Red Shoes* on all-day and half-day sails, we came to the conclusion that they were making much more money than we were, with half the work. Since this was to be their last year of chartering, we decided we would try to fill the void the following summer.

Warm weather never stays long in Maine, and soon the hotels and restaurants began boarding up their windows. There was a nip in the air, one that we had not felt since our maiden voyage in May. When October came, we started migrating southward, coming to roost at our old spot alongside the Barton Machine Shop barge on the Piscataqua River. We had not made enough money to survive the winter, so I began to think about job possibilities.

One day I met George Gendron, a young man who worked on one of the Portsmouth fishing boats. We talked about sailing to the Caribbean and I mentioned my thoughts about a film and the need for investors. Although he had little money to invest, he knew others who he thought might be interested. Before long, we had four people willing to invest in a film and sail to the West Indies with us. Anne Sauve and Burt Richardson had both recently finished college. Anne was involved in dance and mime. Burt was an aspiring young author. Both were from the Portsmouth area, as was Dave Mann, the manager of Valle's Steak House in Kittery, Maine. Glen Doherty, a mechanical engineer and designer of audio equipment, was from Massachusetts.

At this point, Doris and I had been engaged for more than a year, and we felt it was a good time to firm things up. On November 9, we got our families together and my father, a Baptist minister, conducted a short service aboard *Appledore,* tied up to the float alongside Doris's father's pier in Kittery. But I had miscalculated the depth, and as the tide dropped to dead low, *Appledore* started listing to starboard. As guests arrived, they looked at me dubiously, but by noon, the tide had come up enough to refloat her.

Having been so busy for the previous four weeks getting ready to sail south, neither of us had given much thought to clothing, or even to our wedding night. I wore a gray sweater and a clean pair of pants. Relatives were happy to see that at least I had found time to shave. Doris had not planned on wearing a special outfit, but some friends were determined she was not going to wear blue jeans. Many times we were reminded that this would be one of the most important days in our lives. They finally agreed on a pink blouse and white pants. We had shared so much the previous year that, with or without the ceremony, we already felt we were united. Once the ceremony and small reception were over, I felt relieved. Now I could get back to readying the boat. Departure day was only five days away. Doris's friends were appalled. Were we really going to sleep aboard the boat with the crew? Doris shrugged. They took up a collection and presented us with the key to a room in the local Holiday Inn. The next morning, the desk clerk called, as I had asked, to wake us up at 7:00 a.m. I hustled Doris out of the hotel and back to the boat. She looked perturbed: "You could at least have treated me to breakfast. I feel like I just married *Appledore* instead of you!" I reminded her that few people get a six-month honeymoon to the West Indies!

Herb and Doris, just married. Boutilier photo.

Appledore's First Voyage

We left Kittery on November 14. The wind was blowing out of the southeast at 15 knots with higher gusts to 25 knots. We had left at slack water, but by the time we reached the mouth of the Piscataqua River, the tide had turned and a swift current was running out against the wind. A heavy chop had formed, making for an uncomfortable situation. There seemed little point in trying to beat all night against a strong southeast breeze, so we sailed to Appledore Island and anchored for the night, hoping for a more favorable breeze the next day.

By 5:00 a.m., the wind had shifted to the northwest at 20 knots and we were off and running. Twelve hours later, we reached the entrance to the Cape Cod Canal. Like the Piscataqua River, the canal has a strong current, and we were forced to wait at the entrance for the current to slacken. Boats are not supposed to go through the canal without an engine, so we were glad for the cover of darkness.

Late the next day, we had tacked to Newport, Rhode Island, where we stayed several days securing odds and ends and waiting for the breeze to become more favorable for sailing south.

On November 19, we were underway from Newport. Three days later we were thirtly miles off Atlantic City, New Jersey and becalmed.

This was one of the first times since I had begun sailing *Appledore* that I wished I had had an engine. Until this point, we had gotten by with sail alone except for an occasional assist from the skiff and Seagull outboard. Offshore, we rolled so heavily that the skiff would have been in constant danger of swamping. At noon, the wind was still light and variable, but I knew the fast-falling barometer promised heavy weather. At this point, though, I still expected a gale at worst. With an engine, we might have motored into the nearest port of refuge, but without it and with a wind too light to make much progress, we were at the mercy of Mother Nature.

As the afternoon wore on, I looked with dread at the barometer, wishing it were malfunctioning. It had dropped from 29.9 inches at noon to 29.4 inches by 5:30 p.m., a sure sign of approaching strong winds. I listened to the weather forecast on my portable radio, hoping my fears were groundless. In the late afternoon, storm warnings were posted. (Storm warnings mean winds of 48 knots and above.) I had been in storms while on Coast Guard icebreakers and in the Merchant Marine, so I knew a little of what to expect. What I failed to realize was that 20-foot seas viewed from the bridge of an icebreaker 35 feet off the water are very different from 20-foot waves viewed from the deck of *Appledore* 4 feet off the water.

By midnight, the seas had built to 15 feet, with a steady wind of 40 knots. Spray blew across the boat, continually drenching the helmsman. The hatches and splashboards were put in and shut, making it dark and stuffy below decks. Each hour the southwest wind increased. With the temperature in the low 30s, steering became a cold and difficult task. Quartering waves were also making it a real battle. A half-hour watch meant exhaustion. The spray had found hundreds of avenues around the hatches to seep below and make life more miserable. No one's bunk was spared.

I had heard several different arguments about what to do in a storm. Some yachtsmen advocate heaving-to, lowering sails, staying below, battening the hatches, and leaving the vessel to the mercy of the wind and seas. Others advise running with the seas at your back, making sure not to let the seas catch you on the beam lest they roll the boat over. I had never been able to decide which procedure was most effective, so I was willing to experiment with both. At first light, we tied the helm over, went below, and waited to see what would happen. The only sounds were the whistling of the wind when we sat atop a wave and the crash of the waves as they crested and slammed against *Appledore's* hull. There was no talk. Everyone huddled in their wet bunks, trying to stay warm. Under the circumstances, the crew was excellent, everybody doing his or her best to help get us through. I never sensed a feeling of fear from the crew, although I could feel a lot of eyes staring at me, trying to access my thoughts.

It was unbelievably cold below decks, because our stoves were useless. The wind created such a downdraft that the smoke would force us back up on deck. All our lights were kerosene, and only a few were gimbaled. With everything buttoned up tightly, we were in no position to compete with these archaic oil lamps for air, so the interior remained dark and cold. The cabin sole was a sorry sight: clothes, raingear, and an assortment of personal items strewn everywhere. Glen's bunk in the forepeak was pitching so violently (not to mention being soaked) that he had finally forsaken it, throwing his bedding on the main cabin sole and making the most of it there. The galley was downright dangerous. A gallon of Wesson Oil had broken loose, making it a skating rink. I hung on for dear life while trying to consult my charts. Add to that a bottle of French dressing and a box of Tide and you get one indescribable mess. We all tried to clean it up but never were able to remove a last thin film of the oil. Even Smitty, our seafaring cat, was having a hard time. She would sit by her flooded litter box and howl. There was nothing we could do about pumping it out.

We were hove-to only a couple of hours when a particularly large wave broke over the beam, heeling us over on our starboard side. Then came a thunderous sound; the wood in the cabintops crackled and we could hear the crash of dozens of items as they were wrenched out of their storage spaces and tossed onto the cabin sole. Slowly the boat began to right herself. So much for heaving-to. "God helps those who help themselves." I decided that if we were going to drown, it would not be with us lying on our backsides waiting for disaster to strike.

Down came the staysail and up went the storm jib, and at noon we came about to run before the increasing seas. There was not much to see except the two huge mountains of water on either end of us. Every other wave was cresting and breaking. Large plumes of water caught our stern and cascaded over the already miserable helmsman. Somehow I managed to get some film footage for our "romantic Caribbean islands video." That was a laugh.

We were making a good 10 knots, surfing on the crests of the waves. It made surfing in Hawaii look tame. As we descended into the troughs, the wind would ease off, the mountains of water blocking us from its full velocity. But as we rose slowly, foot by foot, we could feel the wind begin to take hold once again, until it reached a crescendo on the top of the crest and shook the mast with punishing force. We had stopped trying to differentiate the rain from the spray, for it all came at us as one. We were now headed north toward Block Island — back where we had come from.

The seas continued to build, but we had by this time stopped trying to judge their height. To us, there were only two kinds: those we rode over uneventfully and those that crested and wreaked havoc on deck. The cold had begun to weaken us.

An uneventful hour passed with very few waves breaking over us. The air was still bitterly cold, and it was easy to let down our defenses. While I steered, Doris huddled in the corner of the cockpit, her icy hands tucked up in her slicker for warmth. Darkness had been with us for a couple of hours, so we were no longer watching the waves. In fact, we had been talking about what port we would make and what we would do when we got there. We agreed that a motel room with a hot bath was a must. Suddenly, out of the blackness, came one monstrous wave. It came up so quickly and quietly, not having curled or broken yet, that I had no time to warn Doris.

I braced myself as the wave cascaded over our port quarter, heeling us onto our starboard side. I could not see Doris; I had all I could do to hold onto the wheel, as water flowed in rivers across my body. When the worst had passed, I looked for Doris, but she was gone.

I groped frantically through the darkness, looking for my bride of only two weeks, It was a long minute before I found her on the starboard side, where she had come up against the lifelines. She was still partly submerged. I could see her arms and legs flailing as she tried to untangle herself from the lifelines and come up for air. It was a blessing that the line on her life harness held, or she probably would have been washed overboard. And there would have been no way to tack back against those waves.

In her log, Doris wrote:

We'd been sitting discussing our next port, my concern being just what port it would be. If this kept up too long, we would end up in Canada somewhere. Although Herb was trying to give me encouragement and assuring me it would not last that long, I was not convinced. It already seemed an eternity.

The lack of food plus the cold were sapping our reserves. As I sat in the corner of the cockpit, I was more concerned with keeping some sense of feeling in my fingers than in the seas; thus it came as a complete surprise when this wave hit. It felt as if a huge hand had hit me in the back, propelling me forward. I felt pain as my knee hit the edge of the cockpit combing and I continued forward in a somersault and came to rest on the deck. I was completely under water. Compared to the air, the water felt warm. I do not remember fear, just surprise. As the initial shock passed, I found myself groping for air. Luckily, the water had begun to recede, and I easily got my head above the surface. I could feel the water running down my back. It no longer felt warm. I looked over and saw Herb rushing toward me and I was overjoyed to see him. I wanted to ask him again when he thought this storm would end and where we would finally make port but decided not to.

At dusk, we could see the light from Fire Island Inlet on the horizon; at 11:00 p.m., we picked up Montauk Light. The wind had climaxed and was dying.

In the morning, we were coming up on Block Island, not making very good progress toward Newport. We needed some drive and started sewing the clips back on the mainsail. Soon we were ready to take off the trysail and rehoist the main, after which we picked up speed. Around midnight, we anchored in Newport, Rhode Island, a tired but happy crew.

Nor had all that cold been imaginary. The next morning, there was a dusting of snow on the deck.

Friends and relatives were overjoyed to hear from us, fearing as they followed the storm's progress that we had been lost at sea. My brother, Steve, then a Coast Guardsman stationed in Philadelphia, reported that they had had a day of steady 60-knot winds.

During the morning, we collected every stitch of clothing we owned and hired a taxi to get us to the nearest laundry. There we proceeded to fill all 20 machines. At this time of year, Newport usually is deserted, so there were surprised looks on the faces of local users who unfortunately chose that particular day to do their laundry. One old gent left muttering to himself, "Don't tell me those damned tourists are back already."

Because of our harried start, I feared we might lose some of our crew. They showed their mettle, however, and we left Newport on December 5 with all hands on board.

The hours of daylight went by smoothly, and we made good speed ahead of a northwest wind. After dark, however, a squall hit us with 35-knot winds driving a blizzard of snow into our faces. Fortunately, it did not last long.

December 12 found us entering Chesapeake Bay, a month after we had first left Newport. We had finally been able to clear a large hurdle, a feat which did wonders for crew morale.

Ten days later, we arrived in Morehead City, North Carolina, from where we would head offshore. We were rather reluctant to leave the protection of the waterway. Despite strong winds at times, we had had relatively calm waters thanks to the narrow strip of land between the channel and the Atlantic Ocean, which protected us from the large ocean swells created by countless storms off Cape Hatteras. It was also reassuring to have the option of staying at anchor if the winds were against us. Dawn was always a special time here. The landscape had a serene beauty as the misty morning sun rose over the marsh grass glistening with crystals of frost. The cries of osprey sounded sharp and clear in the crisp morning air. It made us feel good to be alive and sailing.

We stayed in Morehead City until December 29, having decided to spend Christmas ashore rather than at sea and to await some good weather. After calling the National Weather Service for forecasts, we finally received a report that there were five lows in the area, some coming, some going, but the wind would be favorable for a couple of days.

It took us 10 days to sail the 1,200 miles to Antigua, with great winds most of the way. Once we crossed the Gulf Stream, there were several days when we were under full sail, including our large fisherman, and we never had to trim a sail.

On January 9, we picked up the lighthouse on Sandy Island, five miles west of St. Johns, Antigua. We tacked into the harbor, dropping our anchor at 4:00 a.m. The temperature was already 80°, and a gentle breeze blew toward us from the island, carrying with it heady aromas from the local rum factory, island vegetation, and the smoldering charcoal that burned next to many of the islanders' shacks. After having smelled nothing but salt air for more than a week, we found the scents particularly intoxicating. As darkness dissolved to daylight, we were in the midst of a beautiful aquamarine pool. For the crew members who had never been to a tropical island before, it would leave a lasting impression.

The next day, we started sailing down the coast to English Harbour, Antigua's yachting center. Along the way we stopped in Deep Bay, a beautiful quiet cove about four miles from St. Johns. There were no other boats or even houses, only a lovely white-sand beach and the remains of a sunken vessel surrounded by brightly colored fish. It became our favorite anchorage, and we returned to it often to relax and shoot film footage.

English Harbor has many interesting yachts, including several million-dollar beauties, but the one that interested me the most was named *Eric the Red*. A flimsy boat of about 21 feet, it was built of plywood and miscellaneous scrap materials. The sails were the remains of other yachts' tattered sails, although I was told that at one time the owner had used a triple thickness of bedsheets. Nonetheless, the boat had made three transatlantic crossings. After her second crossing, she had been placed in a maritime museum in England, but it was not long before the owner, Donald Ridler — a tall blond young man — got itchy to sail again and took her out of storage, hoping not only to sail across the Atlantic but also to cross the Pacific. Before he left for Panama, Doris and I went aboard *Eric the Red*. There was little stability, the two of us having to position ourselves on either side of the boat lest she tip her rail in the water. I offered the young owner some of our extra building supplies and wished him good luck. We were told later that *Eric the Red* met her end in the Pacific. As with singlehanded sailor Bill Dunlop and his tiny vessel, the monstrous Pacific Ocean swallowed her up, leaving no trace.

Sailing from island to island without an engine might have been difficult except that at this time of year the Caribbean is blessed with a strong breeze called the Christmas winds. They are particularly strong in

Appledore I, *off St. Lucia.*

January and February, often reaching 40 knots. Many passages were extremely rough and uncomfortable, but the breezes provided the power we needed to sail up and down the chain of islands swiftly.

In Antigua, we met Donald Street, author of *A Cruising Guide to the Lesser Antilles* — the Bible for many sailors in these waters. Don was an interesting character. Becoming fed up with modern aids for mariners — particularly his boat's auxiliary engine — he had removed the motor and committed it to the briny deep, pledging that the only way to sail was by sail alone. He looked contemptuously at yachts that motorsailed. *Appledore*, having no engine, attracted his attention. In our book, he wrote: "To the crew of *Appledore*, I am glad someone else believes in straight sail, good luck, good sailing and don't install an engine." I was young and new enough at sailing that I swallowed it all up. I do admire people who sail without engines. In our sailing years, we have met several of them — including Mary Maynard Drake, who with her husband and children sailed their boat around the world, and Lin and Larry Pardey, well-known authors. It is a great challenge to travel only by sail, but if you have a tight schedule, it helps to have auxiliary power. An engine also provides a sense of security, a defense against Nature's fickle ways.

On February 16, we left Antigua to visit the island of Montserrat; Bourg des Saintes, a small village in Guadeloupe; and Dominica.

Dominica has been called "the island of running water," supposedly because there is one stream for every day of the year and, in some parts of the island, one rain squall for every hour of the day.

In Roseau, the capital, we anchored in front of the Anchorage Hotel, where the management was extremely hospitable and offered us free showers and the use of their pool and restaurant. From here, we hired a car to take us to Trafalgar Falls, a beautiful 300-foot cascade. We also took a tour to the Carib Reservation, home of the few surviving members of the once-warlike Carib Indian tribe. The first cannibals Europeans had ever seen, the Caribs once ruled most of the islands in the Caribbean, resisting European settlement.

I was quickly falling in love with this wild, untamed little island. The extremely mountainous topography had kept the sugar lords from denuding the island of its virgin forests, unlike many of the smaller, flatter islands in the Lesser Antilles.

In Portsmouth, Dominica, I obtained permission to film the workers on the Geest banana plantation, where men and women worked from sunup till sundown, earning as little as $1.00 a day carrying 75-pound stalks of bananas on their heads out of the fields. Witnessing this poverty, we found it easy to see why there was so much racial hatred. The management had allowed me to film, but at my own risk. I cannot say I felt too secure. On Friday, when the ship came to pick up the boxes of bananas for shipment to England, I went to photograph the loading process. At least a hundred women were scurrying like ants, carrying boxes from the sheds to the lighters that transferred the bananas out to the ship. Most of the women ignored me, but several did not, and at one point I found myself surrounded by a group of angry women. I had begun to fear what might happen to my camera equipment when Doris elbowed her way through the crowd. She defused the situation immediately. "Is this your man?" they asked contemptuously. With a sigh and a look of resignation, Doris admitted I was. I do not know whether or not they felt sorry for her, but they then decided to ignore me while questioning Doris about our relationship and why we did not have children. But time is money, and it was not long before they raced back to continue carrying the boxes.

Fort-de-France, Martinique, was our next stop. Being a French island, it was much more affluent than its English counterparts. As an overseas department of France, the people are entitled to French welfare, and it certainly made a difference. In fact, it had the highest standard of living in the Caribbean. As usual, we hired a cab to see the major attractions. Because of the film, we were forcing ourselves to see more of the islands than we would ever have considered had it been strictly a vacation. We discovered that we enjoyed getting off the beaten path and mixing with the working folk. Often, one or more of the crew would accompany us.

Our final stop in Martinique was Saint Pierre, a city that had been destroyed in 1902 by the eruption of Mt. Pelée, killing 30,000 people. Only two people survived, one of whom was a criminal who had been locked in a jail cell. The ruins are still there, nestled among the modern homes.

A few days later, we anchored in Saint Lucia, another lush, mountainous island. Our favorite anchorage has always been the Pitons, a small bay enclosed on each side by two 2,000-foot lava plugs. The plugs are all that remain of a weathered-away volcanic crater. The beach in this bay falls off abruptly to 80 feet, so the usual method of anchoring here is to put out a stern anchor and tie the bow line to one of the hundreds of coconut palms that are part of a plantation. The main disadvantage of this particular anchorage is its "williwaws" (strong downdrafts of air that shoot straight down from the plugs). We were buffeted by 40-knot gusts while we stayed there. Yet the spot is uniquely beautiful, and it was peaceful and unspoiled. The only dwelling belonged to the caretaker, Mr. Andrews, whom we got to know and like. He allowed us to take some of the green coconuts, called jelly nuts. There is no more refreshing drink than the milk from one of these nuts.

From Saint Lucia, it was on to Saint Vincent, where everyone but Anne trekked the six miles up La Soufrière to see its crater. The scene was spectacular, with sheer walls of rock descending a hundred feet to the crystal-blue lake below, where a lava plug in the center emits clouds of steam. The heat, steepness, and distance left us exhausted, and after the third reenactment of the final climb to the top for motion picture footage, I feared mutiny. Meanwhile, Anne, aboard *Appledore*, was approached by a boatload of men who wanted to know whether she was alone. Luckily, she thought quickly and told them her boyfriend was below decks.

When we arrived in Grenada, *Appledore* was hauled out at Grenada Yacht Services. Her hull looked good for the miles she had traveled. While she was up on the ways, Doris and I visited one of the island's nutmeg plantations. One-third of the world's nutmeg is produced in Grenada. The entire crew paid a visit to the Nutmeg Restaurant and Bar to sample their famous nutmeg ice cream, but after one dish, we were content to stick to the local Carib beer.

From Grenada, it was back up the archipelago to Union Island, Carriacou, Bequia, Dominica, and finally Antigua.

It had been a long time since we had had steak or roast beef. In Portsmouth, Dominica, Doris and I passed a store that had a freezer full of meat for sale. But you never know what you might be buying in these small ports, so we resisted the temptation. Back at the boat, we mentioned it to the crew. Dave, who had been in the restaurant business for a long time, said he would check it out. Later that morning, he came back with a beautiful-looking, frozen 5-pound roast. As we put the roast on the counter to defrost, we were in a party mood. Doris and I went off to film for a few hours and get some wine. When we returned, we descended the hatch to check the meat and were met by a sickening odor. We could not have been more disappointed. Dave insisted the meat was all right, that it was their method of slaughter and preparation. We cooked the roast, but the smell emanating from the oven was not encouraging. When the meat was put on the table, there was only silence. Most of us expected it to get up and walk away. Still Dave defended the meat and offered to cut it. No takers. By this time, he was quite angry with us, so he cut off a large piece and began to eat it. Still no other takers. We then began to speculate what kind of animal it came from. Most of us agreed that it must be either horse or donkey, and we wondered whether we would hear Dave braying during the night. Dave finally conceded defeat, and the roast was thrown to the fish. (On later trips around the world, this would happen many more times.)

Our return stop in Antigua was brief, most of it spent relaxing in Deep Bay. It was April and almost time to head home. I put away the camera equipment and enjoyed snorkeling over a shipwreck, a coal ship that had caught fire and sunk at the turn of the century. We carried scuba tanks on board but rarely used them, since it was such a bother to have them filled.

By now, the Christmas winds had faded to a light gentle breeze that did little to cool the land by day. Evenings were a relief. It was totally relaxing to sit in a comfortable chair at the Galley Bay Surf Club with a Carib beer and listen to the crickets, the pounding of waves on the beach, and the tinkling of small pebbles and shells in the receding surf. The only feature that detracted from the scene was a guard dressed in a trench coat and wide-brimmed hat pulled low over his eyes. Brandishing a machete, he tested its sharpness on the limbs of nearby trees. I suppose he was there to reassure the guests.

We left Antigua for the last time on April 8, stopping briefly at Nevis, Saint Kitts, and Saba. Saba, a volcanic Dutch island ringed with steep walls, has no anchorages to speak of. A small pier juts out from a relatively unprotected anchorage. Saba was a relief from the busy, tension-filled British islands. Here we met Del Bunker, an American who was living on the island. He had worked hard to help the local people, sending many islanders — especially children who needed special surgery — to the United States for treatment. He tried to encourage community projects, even a soapbox derby. Considering the steepness of the roads, that was an ambitious undertaking. He made our stay very pleasant by taking us on a tour of the island and allowing us to use his cottage.

In Saint Martin, our last stop in the West Indies, we met another yacht that would change our lives. *Souwester* was a 60-foot wooden schooner from Nova Scotia. I was very impressed with the space below, which added steam to my dream of a larger *Appledore*. What interested me more, however, was the fact that the *Souwester* took a paying crew on extended cruises. This set me to thinking . . . .

Appledore I
*sailing off
Key West.*

Hard Times, Good Times

In May we were back home from the West Indies and in another financial crisis. In 10 days, we had to pay monthly installments to two banks. The rest of the crew had returned to their previous jobs and interests.

"I told you this was going to happen," Doris informed me. "Now what are we going to do?"

"Beneficial Finance," I replied. They had come through before; perhaps they would again. The company kept sending me a card that offered instant credit: "Just take the card into any office worldwide and for 30 days you can borrow up to $1,000 without charge." It went on to say that I was a preferred customer. I went in for the loan. At Beneficial, I was familiar with the procedure and asked for the manager.

"He's busy, sir."

"I'll wait. It's important," I replied.

"May I ask what it is in regards to, sir?"

"Borrowing money on this card," I said.

Finally the manager was free. "Yes, Mr. Smith, may I help you?"

I stood up and we shook hands. "Yes, I am one of your preferred customers and I have this card that entitles me to borrow up to $1,000 for 30 days at no cost. Is there a catch to it?"

He asked to see the card. "Come in and sit down, Mr. Smith. How much would you like to borrow?"

"A thousand dollars," I told him.

"What will the money be used for?" he asked.

"To pay two other loans that I have with banks."

"You mean you want to close them out?" he asked.

"No, just make the monthly installments," I said.

"And how do you expect to repay us the $1,000 in 30 days?"

I would have liked to tell him that I did not have any idea how I

41

was going to pay it off in 30 days. And I failed to explain that my wife was pregnant and we had no insurance. Instead, I mentioned that I had a 48-foot schooner and expected to be getting some money soon from chartering it.

I got the loan and returned to the boat feeling quite good about it. "Doris, I have fantastic news. I got the $1,000 loan. Let's go out to eat."

"But Herb, now we have three loans to pay back."

"No problem. We will be chartering next week," I assured her.

We sailed down to Boothbay Harbor, and a week before Memorial Day, I had 12,000 brochures printed. "Sail aboard *Appledore*," they said, "just back from her West Indies adventure." I distributed them all around Boothbay Harbor and we picked up some business. Before long, many more vacationers came to Maine and we managed to make enough money to pay the bills. I was also able to convert the $1,000 Beneficial loan to a two-year note, and we stayed one step ahead of our next payments.

The summer of 1976 started well. Although we still did not have the luxury of an auxiliary diesel engine, we managed to operate three scheduled trips a day from Boothbay's Spruce Point Inn. To augment the business, Captain Eliot Winslow let us book our trips out of the *Argo* ticket booth at Fisherman's Wharf. The *Argo* cruise boat takes as many as 150 people at a time on scenic tours of the outlying islands. In August, we found ourselves booked several days in advance, and, by the end of the summer, we had saved enough money to install a small engine. Then we headed south to Key West, Florida, to try our hand at chartering there.

It was important to get to Key West fairly soon, because Doris was 7 months pregnant, so we ended up departing Boothbay Harbor on the worst day of the year. The wind was coming out of the south at 30 knots, which put it right on the nose, and a 6-foot sea was making into the harbor. The next day, we had to be in Kittery to pick up the three crew members who would share the expenses with us on our trip to Florida. We were joined by Paul Mathews, a retired Navy chief; his 20-year-old daughter, Paula; and young Larry Smith, a midwesterner who had been roaming the country looking for excitement.

Not wanting to risk a repeat of the storm we had experienced off the coast of New Jersey in 1974, we decided to sail in close along the coast, using inland waterways as often as we could. On November 16, we passed through an awakening New York City. As darkness faded, we could see early risers jogging in a park and the fleet of yellow cabs whisking people to unknown destinations. As we passed the Statue of Liberty, we all stood on deck. The green weathered lady standing gaunt against a dramatic dawn sky stirred deep thoughts. Flickers of sunlight played off her arms and crown, and I thought of all the people who had sailed by her through the years. Among them were famous singlehanded sailors such as Alain Gerbault in 1924 aboard *Firecrest* and Ed Allcard in 1948 aboard *Temptress*.

In Norfolk, Virginia, my sister, Rachel, cosigned yet another bank loan. It was discouraging to see how quickly our indebtedness was increasing. But when you are young, it does not seem to ruin too many nights' sleep. You keep believing that everything will work out in the next month or two. You might even win the sweepstakes. I had given Doris a sweepstakes ticket for her birthday in October, but I don't think she was too impressed.

Except for the loss of our cats, the trip down the waterway was uneventful. Smitty never could get used to our new engine. She shook and howled every time we turned it on. During our stay in Point Judith, Rhode Island, she went ashore and never returned. Not even a large reward could bring her back. To make matters worse, her kitten fell overboard one night in South Carolina. She had started climbing the ratlines, the rope ladder to the top of the mast, and I think her lack of balance led to her demise. Although Doris said very little about it, I knew she was crushed, so in Isle of Hope, South Carolina, I started looking for a kitten. A dock man at the marina assured me he had just the replacement, although he warned me it had lacked care. At six months old, it fit in the palm of my hand. It was basically all head and eyes and its small body was alive with fleas. I was not sure I wanted to keep it, but once Doris saw it, she was determined to help it. We thought of many names, but Bones was the one that stuck with him. I could well imagine how it had survived; a feistier cat was never born. By eight months, it was full size, still not much bigger than a kitten. What he lacked in size, however, he made up in sheer courage. Although we had gotten rid of the fleas and he had grown a beautiful black coat, we could do nothing to correct his bowleggedness, which caused him to weave back and forth as he made his way down the dock. He looked like a sailor coming back from his first night of shore leave.

Paul had to be back in Maine by December 1, so he left us in South Carolina. Although he had dreamed of shirt-sleeve weather, he was never able to take off his winter jacket. The year 1976 had had one of the coldest autumns in history. Even as we sailed into Florida, the air was frosty. I began to think that the Florida of oranges and bikinis was a myth. By Vero Beach, we finally began to feel some warm air, and palm trees became more numerous. Finally, we were able to shed our long johns and soak up the sun's rays.

We arrived in Key West on a cool, overcast morning. Since we would be sailing to and from the marina several times a day, we got an outside slip. Even then, a lot of restoration had been done in the downtown area. Once we began to explore the island, we liked it more and more.

I paid a visit to the Coast Guard and received some bad news. I would have to have 30 days of sailing experience in Florida waters before they would issue me a license to carry passengers. It meant no charters and thus no money until January. Meanwhile, marina fees began to eat into our little cash, and I still had to fly to Miami to take the Coast Guard local- knowledge test. At first, I considered hitchhiking, but that would have taken too long; it would take only six hours if I flew. The airfare cleaned us out, but our good friend Dave Mann offered to help us out, and he sent a few hundred dollars. I was reluctant to ask for it, since it would mean five loans to repay, but with Doris expecting the baby any day, I borrowed the money gratefully.

We had figured the baby was due sometime in the first two weeks of January. I had asked Doris to see a doctor, but her reply had been, "What are they going to tell me, that I am pregnant?" Physically she felt fine and the baby was active, so we assumed everything was okay.

While waiting for the 30 days to pass, I had 12,000 brochures printed. By now I had learned some of the tricks of the distribution trade. We also hired an answering service to take reservations. Meanwhile, we put *Appledore* up for sale, with plans to build a larger vessel for sailing around the world. Bud McIntosh began to draw up the plans. At this point, the tension must have been getting to me, because I let down my guard and became ill. A virus had gotten into my lungs, Camel cigarettes were out for a while. I went to the public health hospital outpatient clinic for some treatment. It was a cool day when I hitched a ride in from Kings Point, but I was perspiring profusely by the time I arrived.

At the clinic, I told the doctor my symptoms and my problems. "My wife is pregnant and expecting any day now."

"Oh, that's nice. Will it be your first?" he asked.

"Yes."

"Who is her doctor?" he asked.

"She hasn't been to see one since she became pregnant. She started getting bigger and missed her period about nine months ago."

"Where is she now?" he asked.

"Back on board the boat," and, I added for drama, "I hope she isn't having it right now." He gave me a peculiar look. For the previous few weeks, I had never ventured far from the boat because I thought Doris might need me in a hurry. We were not planning to deliver the baby ourselves on board, although Doris once had brought up that idea. The hospital was only a mile from the marina, and I had every intention of taking Doris there. I mentioned Doris's pregnancy to the public health doctor because I had heard a rumor that if a woman was a bona fide crew member aboard a U.S.-documented commercial passenger-carrying vessel or fishing boat, she would be entitled to public health services. At the clinic, the doctor took this into consideration and asked to see my document, which I had brought in order to get admittance myself. It said: "*Appledore*, commercial passenger-carrying sailing vessel."

"Are you the captain?" he asked.

"Yes," I replied.

"And your wife is your only crew member?"

"Yes, she is my first mate."

"Well, I don't see any problem. Have her come in to see me this afternoon."

I rushed back to the boat and told Doris the good news that she could receive public health services, but she was not very impressed.

"Where is this place?" she asked.

"Downtown."

"What kind of a clinic is it?"

"It's a nice place and a good doctor," I replied. "It's where all the seamen go from the shrimp boats."

"Did he say how much it would cost?"

"Yes. It doesn't cost anything if you are a crew member on a commercial boat. Now come on. Let's get going before they close."

Just then Doris stood up and clutched her stomach. I thought it was too late. "What's the matter?" I asked worriedly.

"Nothing."

"Is it coming?"

"Not yet. Believe me, you will be the first to know," she assured me. "By the way, what did you tell the doctor, exactly?"

"Don't worry, I just told him you were nine months pregnant. I did mention it was possible you could be in labor."

"You didn't!" she said incredulously. "How could you say that? I feel foolish enough already."

When we walked into the clinic, I mentioned to the doctor that it was not easy getting Doris there because she was a little skeptical about doctors. He looked at us in surprise. Obviously I had not exaggerated much. There sat Doris in a pink blouse and maternity jeans looking all of nine months pregnant. A wisp of hair fell over her forehead. If size alone was the determining factor, she was ready to deliver at any moment.

Perhaps he took my comment about her skepticism a little too seriously, because he was very gentle and patient with his questions. He told us that they were not equipped to handle deliveries but that she would be able to see a Dr. Robinson, an excellent physician who was the chief of

Herb and Tom, two days old.

staff at the local hospital. The nurse came out and handed the doctor a form
to sign, and from that moment on, Doris was well taken care of. Three
weeks later, we were blessed with Thomas James Smith. Dr. Robinson and I
received him from the womb at 4:00 a.m. on January 20, 1977. It was the
same day that Jimmy Carter was sworn in as our thirty-ninth president.

Two days later, Doris and Tommy were back on board. We had a
charter scheduled for one hour after I picked them up from the hospital.
When the passengers showed up, I got the schooner underway myself
and told them that Doris had just had a baby, was down below cleaning
up, and would be up shortly. The expressions on the passengers' faces
were ones of utter amazement. Perhaps they misunderstood me and
thought she had just that moment given birth. They offered to come back
at another time, since Tommy then began to express his hunger pangs.

When Doris did appear, I said, "Why don't you take it easy today, Doris?" Doris looked at me and made a face as if to say, "Oh, aren't you generous!" So it all began — a very special winter in Key West.

We were soon getting a lot of business by going out with anyone at any time. It was hard work, and we had to time our departures so that Tommy was just fed and put in his cradle on the floor, wedged between the table and the bunk. At one of Tommy's checkups, the pediatrician asked if she was imagining things or did the baby really have a tan.

Just as the season was coming to a close, a buyer came to look at *Appledore*. After having it surveyed, he bought it for $56,000. We were rich! What a pleasure it was to deliver her up the coast to the Sassafras River in the Upper Chesapeake Bay without having to worry about money. We walked away and never looked back. From there we went directly to Bud McIntosh's house in Dover, New Hampshire, to pick up the plans for our next schooner. After paying off our five loans, we were in a good position to apply for a $100,000 bank loan to build *Appledore II*.

Appledore II, *under construction, Gamage Shipyard.*

A Commercial Venture

In December 1977, Doris and I and our infant son, Tom, drove through Damariscotta, Maine, with everything we owned piled in the back of our pickup truck. We were on our way to South Bristol, Maine, where *Appledore II* was going to be built. Originally, we had intended to build the new schooner in Portsmouth, and we had gone so far as to rent a large vacant building, install a 20-inch planer, stockpile some of our oak and pine in the lofts, and line up a couple of men to help.

We had not even begun the construction when there was talk of a pay increase and worker's compensation. Since the boat would be built by the sawn-frame method, something I knew little about, I had inquired at the Gamage Shipyard about a contract for the hull only, never expecting it to be within my budget. The day I received the price of $50,000, I rethought my plans. The amount seemed reasonable, and a gang of men working on the hull could get it done faster, meaning less interest on the loan. The $50,000 did not include the materials, and we would be responsible for fairing the hull, caulking it, installing the engine, finishing the interior, and building the masts and rigging.

As we drove through Damariscotta, we knew right away that we liked this part of Maine. The telephone poles were dressed out in genuine spruce wreaths, Christmas lights hung across the street, and the tires squeaked as they rolled over newly fallen snow. As I stopped on the side of the road to get the ice off the windshield wipers, the wind blew in around the open collar of my shirt. At that moment, it was easy to imagine sailing in the South Pacific.

Our rented house in South Bristol overlooked the Gamage Shipyard, and we had only a short walk to work each morning. We hired part-time babysitters so Doris could accompany me. She was the first woman ever to work in the yard, although a week later they hired a female welder to work on a dragger.

49

Appledore, *nearing completion.*

Prior to arriving in South Bristol, I had tramped the woods of New Hampshire with lumberman Lawrence Lyford. Most boatbuilders were using red oak because of its availability, but it does not have the rot resistance of white oak. Large white-oak logs were becoming scarce in Maine and New Hampshire, so I traipsed through countless woodlots marking (with different-colored ribbons) trees for specific boat timbers. Once the trees were felled, the logs were delivered to Rand Lumber Company in Rye, New Hampshire, where Jim Rand sawed them into the necessary lengths and widths. A trailer truck took them to South Bristol, where I threw them off the truck. When winter had come, with its accompanying snow and ice, I regretted not having stacked them neatly. Many times I had to use a shovel and crowbar to dislodge the wood we would need for the next day.

Our work at the shipyard was challenging and interesting for eight months. Under the direction of the late Harvey Gamage, the shipyard had become famous for building many of the World War II wooden minesweepers and some of the more recent windjammer schooners, including the *Harvey Gamage, Bill of Rights, Shenandoah, Mary Day, Clearwater*, and the arctic research vessel *Hero*.

The machinery had not changed for half a century. Huge ship's bandsaws could cut through a 12-inch white oak timber like a piece of cheese. The team of builders was now headed by Linwood Gamage, Harvey's son, and old-timers such as Earl Haley and Jim McFarland. With the help of Hartwell, Brian, and Pete, they could easily handle the large timbers. Doris and I went home each evening exhausted, while they went out to moonlight on other jobs. Fortunately for us, the shipyard was closed on weekends.

In February 1978, a storm swept the Maine coast, pushing the tides to historic highs. Water entered the building and came up under the keel. Everyone joked about an early launching, but it would be many months before *Appledore* would be ready.

Doris and I had all we could do to keep up with the crew. I had the unenviable job of caulking the hull. When Harvey Gamage was alive, the floor beneath the hull had been dirt. He would spray the hull and floor every week with water to keep the planks from drying and shrinking, but that was a practice lost to the past.

By 1977, the dirt floors were partially sealed with cement, since most of the hulls being built were steel. To make matters worse, the large rear doors were left open to let out smoke from the welding torches and let in the cooling sea breezes. As a result, the planks shrank, and the once tightly fitted seams opened so wide that I could stick my finger into them. Not only did it make caulking difficult, but it also meant that with so much cotton wedged between the two planks, the backs of these seams would never again fit together tightly. Les Thompson, another old-timer who was now retired, showed me how to caulk the boat.

I spent part of my time putting in the butt blocks, pieces of wood that are fastened behind the joints of two planks. Linwood felt that they would not be needed with sawn-frame construction, and if I wanted them, I would have to put them in myself. If I had planned to sail the boat only along the Maine coast, I might have gone along with him, but that was not the kind of cruise I was planning. While I was busy with the butt blocks, caulking, and fairing the hull, Doris was busy plugging the nail holes, puttying the seams, and priming and painting the hull.

Less than a month before we were to launch this *Appledore*, the rudder was built and hung off the sternpost and the steering gear and wheel were installed. When I tried to spin the wheel several times, I barely had the strength to turn it. I refused to buy the theory that it would work itself in and loosen; I knew this had to be changed before we launched the boat.

One day, as I pushed and argued to get it taken off and refitted, one of the workers commented, jokingly, "The only thing we care about is

Greasing the ways for Appledore II.

to see the boat sail around the corner and out of sight. After that, we don't care." I took the "we" to mean "he," but as an image of the Indian Ocean flashed through my mind, I was not laughing. To build a boat and sail it yourself is one thing; to build it for a client may be another matter.

Actually, with the expert knowledge and direction of Linwood, Earl, and Jim, the construction went along well, and I was satisfied with the final product. In August, three days before the yard was to close for summer vacation and seven months after the keel was laid, *Appledore* was ready to be launched.

Launching a schooner in a traditional shipyard is exciting. First they build a cradle under the vessel that rests on wooden planks leading down to the water's edge. The planks then get a heavy coat of grease. On the high tide, when the restraints are cut away from the cradle, the vessel literally slips down the planks and into the water, gaining momentum as it goes. The old-timers say it is not a good launching unless the grease smokes.

On August 22, 1978, Doris christened her *Appledore*, and, with grease smoking, she slid down the ways and into the Atlantic Ocean.

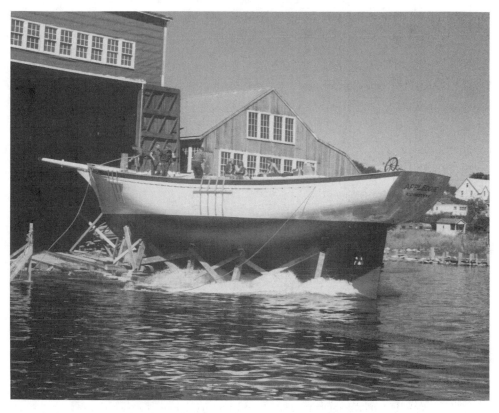

Appledore II, *a perfect launch. Photo by the Reverend Raymond F. Smith.*

In recalling the launching day, Doris wrote:

It was hard to believe *Appledore* was ready for launching. There had been a great deal of speculation during the last month that the work would not be done in time. Linwood challengingly remarked, "If you have your part ready, we will have ours ready." The bets were that we could never get her hull caulked, faired, and painted in time. Herb and I, however, were desperate to get her launched before their vacation. We could not afford to let two precious weeks slip by unproductively, or we would never meet our November deadline for departure on our world trip. It seemed like an impossible task. Before I could begin to fill the seams with putty and paint her hull, Herb had to finish caulking and fairing the hull. In order to give me work, he would drop the caulking and run back to sand a part of the hull he had completed and I would go to work. *Appledore's* hull began to look like a patchwork quilt, with some areas rough and untouched, others sanded, and yet others not only sanded but puttied and painted as well. Forgetting our lunch breaks and working during the extra hour it took Linwood to lock up the shop, I somehow managed to get the last coat of bottom paint on the day before the launch.

We had not sent out too many invitations; we simply did not have the time, so we were surprised to see nearly 1,000 people lined up around South Bristol to watch the launch. Herb had sent a quick note to Bill Alexander, the owner of the Rockport-based windjammer *Timberwind*, and when we saw the gaff-rigged sails of a large sailing vessel come around the bend in the Damariscotta River, we assumed it was Bill. We watched one set of sails after another come into view, until eight of those beautiful Maine ships were anchored expectantly in front of the pier.

It was my job and privilege to christen her. Herb believed in the superstition that it was bad luck not to break the bottle of champagne on the first swing: "Doris, remember to put some power behind your swing," and, "Doris, hold the bottle like this." From the amount of coaching I got that morning, I got the impression that he did not trust even me. "Don't worry, Herb, I have a strong arm," I reassured him. "You've made sure of that these last few months."

A couple of musician friends had joined me on the christening platform and were singing and playing to the waiting crowd. Linwood had come over to tell me it would be happening soon and that he would give me a signal. At that moment, I realized that the instruments were going to be drowned in champagne, and in my attempts to get them moved, I missed Linwood, who was frantically trying to get my attention. Out of the corner of my eye, I saw *Appledore* slipping away. Without giving it a second thought, I whacked the bottle on her quickly moving hull knowing that if I missed the first time, there would be no second chance. Linwood, however, was prepared to run after the boat if need be. He had had to do it before at other launchings. My aim was good, and pink champagne gushed from the shattered, ribbon-covered bottle.

As the crowd cheered and the cannons of the windjammer fleet thundered, shivers traveled up and down my spine. A feeling of exhaustion began to seep into my bones. One of the most exciting moments of our lives had come and gone!

We had a great deal of work still to do, but we were well on the way to meeting our November departure date for our round-the-world cruise.

In September, we motored *Appledore* down to Kittery, where we tied her alongside Doris's father's pier. We had hired Kevin and Curtis Shields to build the interior. Kevin had already spent a month with us in South Bristol. In the end, six other local boatbuilders were working with us. A few of the crew members had also arrived early to help get ready for our departure on November 9.

We advertised in *Yankee* magazine for crew members to share the expenses of our world trip. We needed at least 11 people to consider going. In January, Maria and Jack Stiles had come to South Bristol. Retired and in their early sixties, they had already traveled extensively around the world. They lived out of their suitcases and wherever they were was home. They wanted to join us and were the first to sign up. Every month thereafter, we received many letters from interested people, but no one was signing up. It was difficult for most to make such a big commitment, either in cost or in time (18 months).

One Florida man came to visit and stayed with us for a few days. He was in his fifties and smoked a couple of packs of cigarettes a day. He told us he had just been in the hospital and was recovering from pneumonia. We had our doubts about whether he would be strong enough to make the trip, but he was so determined to go that we could not refuse him. He gave us a deposit on the spot for his wife and himself. A few weeks later, he sent us a certified letter. He was dying of cancer and his doctors said he would not last the 18 months. We returned the deposit, feeling sad for him, but this reinforced our determination not to put off our adventures till our kids grew up or we retired.

By April, we had only two people genuinely interested in the voyage, and we were once again out of money. Things looked dismal and I still had to pay off Gamage. Maria and Jack Stiles wanted to know if they should prepare to depart in six months. I told them yes and felt responsible for taking them around the world.

By October, we had talked to several other interested people. Sandy McBeth, an interior decorator from Denver, Colorado, wanted to join us with her 16-year-old son, Greg. She impressed me with her level of commitment. If we accepted her, she would sell her house and come East in October. Greg had not finished high school, but he would complete it on board through a correspondence program.

Eventually we found the 11 crew members. They were nurses, bankers, teachers, students, and retired couples. There was a big age spread, but it all seemed to work.

We covered our first world voyage in our photographic book, *Dreams of Natural Places*. This second book describes our second world

(above) Appledore II *departing for world voyage accompanied by* Audacity, *with skipper Urban Bean. Boutilier photo. (below) Jack and Maria Stiles,* Appledore II *crew and world adventurers.*

Christmas Day, Cape Town.

voyage. The most obvious difference between the two world trips was that on the first circumnavigation we sailed east to west via the Panama Canal. On the second world trip, we also sailed east to west, but this time via the Strait of Magellan at the tip of South America. The routes of the two voyages come together in Tahiti, from which point the ports, with a few exceptions, were much the same.

It's interesting to note what became of our first world crew. Sixteen-year-old Greg Wellstead finished high school on board, was later appointed to the Merchant Marine Academy at Kings Point, New York, and graduated from there. His mother, Sandy, became a social director aboard the *Lindblad Explorer*.

Eighteen-year-old John Richards went on to college and law school in Washington, DC. Anne and Jack Williams, a young couple in their thirties at

Appledore II *returning to Portsmouth harbor. Photo by the Reverend Raymond F. Smith.*

the time, returned to their respective nursing and banking careers. Maggie Rogers, in her early fifties, went back to her farm in Wiscasset, Maine. Rita Kunkle left us early in the trip and did a considerable amount of sailing in the South Pacific. Donna Twombly, a nurse practitioner, moved to Hawaii and continued to work in the medical field. Alan Twombly, a former physical education teacher took up carpentry.

Our cook, Cathy Mahany, had left the trip in Panama, finding the heat and the cooking responsibilities too much to handle. It was not an easy job. Doris took over and worked by herself for a couple of months until we reached Tahiti, where we hired Alexandra Clark, a young girl from California. From then on, she and Doris split the cooking chores. Maria and Jack Stiles left us in Bali, deciding to continue via a less rigorous mode of transportation. After they left us, they continued traveling the world, visiting, among other countries, China, the USSR, and India. Dave and Marion Dash, a retired couple from Boothbay Harbor, Maine, took their places. Mike Johnson, a psychologist from Virginia and an avid sailor, joined us in South Africa. He later sailed around the Horn aboard the yacht *Lord Jim*. We also took on a Canadian named Werner Dumar for a few weeks in the West Indies.

It is noteworthy to mention here that financial problems plagued us during the first world trip. Before we were halfway around the world, money was getting tight, even though the 11 passengers were sharing the expenses. The problem was that their shares were fixed and prepaid before departure, and with the devaluation of the U.S. dollar and my own miscalculations, we were in a financial crisis. Therefore, we decided we had to take half a deposit on the sale of the boat while we were in South Africa. That barely provided enough money to get us home, and a great deal of time during the rest of the voyage was spent on the telephone and in the telegraph office, trying to get the other half of the deposit, but with no success. After we returned, the sale never went through, since the president of the newly formed company that was purchasing the boat had disappeared with all of the investors' money, including the remainder of our deposit. It was a very substantial sum, because ours was not the only property they were trying to purchase. We did, however, borrow some money until we found another buyer. Then we went straight to Bud McIntosh's house for new plans for a smaller schooner. This was to be one that we could more readily afford, maintain, and sail ourselves.

Building the shed for Appledore III.

A Backyard Project

With the plans for building *Appledore III*, a 56-foot wooden schooner that would have a draft of only 6-1/2 feet and could be transported over the road when completed, we moved to Littleton, New Hampshire, 10 miles north of the White Mountains. As a boy, I had climbed Mount Lafayette with my father and camped out under its shadow. After spending so many years at sea, I longed to go back. My father had also been the pastor of the Franconia (New Hampshire) church for a number of years, and he had spoken often of the delights of living in the mountains. Soon I found the same mysterious spiritual power and pleasure of looking up to the mountains capped either in snow or the bluish-purple haze of summer. The people who lived among these giants were terrific. Tommy started public school there and we had a second child, Lisa.

On February 1, 1983, we began to build a plastic shelter. We were in a hurry to get the plastic up before there was too much snow. It had been a mild winter until then, with only a few inches on the ground. Originally, we were going to take our time building the schooner while I worked full time driving a wood-chip trailer truck. This would keep us from having to borrow heavily and getting ourselves deeply in debt again. However, I soon talked myself into believing that time is too precious and that I would rather be sailing and in debt than driving a trailer truck, so I left the trucking job to work full time on the boat.

The construction of the plastic building did not go smoothly. First we nailed a plate across the top of four 18-foot studs and put them up together as a unit.

"Move it aft a little," I told Doris. "No, no, not that way, the other way!"

Crash! Everything fell.

Doris sighed and said, "How am I supposed to know which way

is aft and which is forward? How about north and south, since we are on land?"

"Okay, we can use north and south," I told her.

We picked up the unit of studs again and started to raise it slowly. Doris was on one end and I was on the other.

"Good, move it north a little. Wait! Hold it! You're going the wrong way!"

Crash!

"Sorry, but I forgot to ask which way was north," Doris informed me. Lisa, our two-year-old daughter, was in the back of our Ford station wagon playing contentedly with her toys. She was warm there and Doris could keep an eye on her, although, when the studs came crashing down, we wished we had not parked the car in the middle of the proposed building site. After school, Tommy, then six, played with his trucks in the snow while our dog, Shep, made a nuisance of herself by biting off the leveling string that we had stretched tight for lining up the studs.

Despite an 8-inch snowstorm and bitter cold weather, we were able to get the shell ready for its plastic covering in two weeks. Our plan was to loft, frame, and plank the boat as fast as two people possibly could do it. Then we would spend the following winter finishing up and outfitting so that the boat would be ready to sail in one year. With this in mind, and our entire life savings and our loans at stake, Doris and I worked 10 hours a day, six days a week, for the next 14 months.

Twelve months earlier, we had again tramped through the woods looking for suitable boatbuilding lumber. We had to find our own timber because white oak was retailing for $3 a board foot, a very substantial price for a project that requires 20,000 board feet.

White oak does not grow well in northern New Hampshire, but we found some in the southern part of the state. Again we asked the loggers to bring the logs into the Rand Lumber Mill in Rye. This came to $150 per thousand board feet of wood. Jim Rand did the sawing, as he had done for our two previous *Appledores*, for $100 per thousand board feet, thus bringing the cost to 25 cents a board foot. The cost was even lower than that because we sold the scraps for firewood and the good, clear sapwood to a retailer in Boston. In the end, the white oak we used in *Appledore* cost us practically nothing, so we saved about $55,000.

We obtained the pine for the interior, about 6,000 board feet, the same way. Most of it came from trees on our own land. One big bull pine that we felled had 125 growth rings.

We found the white cedar at a mill in Vermont. However, the Port Orford cedar, a much-superior species, grows only in a small area in Oregon. That we purchased from a wholesale company, Atlantic Marine,

Lisa

in Newcastle, Maine. The Japanese favor this cedar, a fact that has made it very costly. We paid $1,300 for 1,000 board feet, but soon thereafter, the same amount was retailing for more than $3,000. Today it is practically unobtainable on the East Coast. We could have used white cedar or pine for one-quarter of the cost, but they do not have the same strength as Port Orford cedar, even though both are excellent for boatbuilding. Since we were planning to sail *Appledore* around South America and the Cape of Good Hope, where we would experience some of the roughest oceans in the world, we were investing more than just money: Our lives were at stake as well.

We lofted the boat in our 18-by-20-foot garage. There we laid down the lines from the plans that Bud McIntosh had given us.

The keel pattern, the first physical work we did on the boat itself, took four days to build and was 30 feet 7 inches long and 12 inches wide. We used 400 board feet of white pine and sanded and filled even the shallowest of dents to make sure they wouldn't show up in the casting. Concerned about trying to fit the rest of the boat to an uncorrectable iron keel, we fussed to make sure the pattern was straight, and that the two ends were perfectly shaped.

I had arranged for a Vermont trucker to pick up the keel pattern and take it to the Hartly Hunt foundry in Orange, Massachusetts, but when he arrived, we were disappointed to see that it could not lie flat on the truck. Not only that, but the driver was pessimistic about what fate might

Herb's Pinto with the wooden keel pattern.

befall our pristine baby, so we strapped it instead to the roof of our Ford Pinto station wagon. It was a strange sight at best, with the two shapely ends hanging out a good 10 feet forward and aft. The pattern weighed only 250 pounds, but its pearly-white sides would be sure to attract attention. En route, I saw only two police cars, both preoccupied with ticketing speeding motorists. I wondered what their reactions would have been.

In the foundry, the pattern was bedded in sand and removed, and the hollow then was filled with molten iron. It is amazing to see the precision of the resulting keel. Afterward, the bolt holes were drilled. The foundry did an excellent job.

After air-drying the Port Orford cedar for a few months, we decided to stack it in our garage. Doris and I spent many days carrying the 20-foot-long planks inside. It had been a while since we had worked on a boat together, and we had some problems to work out.

As Doris recalls:

> Every time we needed to work together, I would think of "The Odd Couple" or "Mutt and Jeff." Even the simple job of moving lumber was a problem. Herb complained that because of me he had to carry his end like a woman. I argued that it was easier for him to do so than for me to work like a man. Those planks were at least 90 pounds each and we had several hundred yards to cover with one under each arm. I reminded him that our bodies are not shaped quite the same. My bony prominences stick out more on my hips than his. We also could not get our timing right for dropping them, and I was always releasing my end before Herb did his, causing his end to bounce painfully in his hands.

Fitting the stern post knee, with helpers.

The plastic shelter did not keep out the cold on cloudy days, but it did keep us dry. When the sun came out, however, it acted like a greenhouse, trapping a considerable amount of heat. The biggest problem with the plastic building was the sun penetrating and striking the huge oak timbers. It would have caused them to check and crack. To avoid this, we hung blue tarps overhead to shade the construction area. We also put a coat of linseed oil on the oak and applied it liberally to any newly exposed wood.

On April 9, 1983, the 12,400-pound keel was delivered on a private flatbed truck. Everyone except the driver and I cleared out. No one wanted to be on the receiving end if anything went wrong during the unloading. I blocked up to it with oak timbers; then the keel was hydraulically jacked up, and rollers were placed under it. It was then rolled onto the first set of blocks. The truck moved out from under the keel to where the next set of blocks were placed and finally moved out from under the keel entirely. The keel was left about 5 feet off the ground so we could follow the boltholes from the bottom up and thereby accurately drill the corresponding holes in the wooden part of the keel.

We took time out to tap 15 or 20 maple sugar trees and were surprised at how many gallons of sap it took to produce a cup of thick maple syrup. Unfortunately, we decided to boil it in the house, and soon our ceilings were coated with a sticky brown substance, and the kitchen and dining room wallpaper started to peel away from the wall. Doris was

Roughing out a scarf with a chain saw.

delighted. Now she would get to replace the paper after all. I hated to think about the real cost of those 4 gallons.

Back at the boat, we set up the wooden molds on top of the backbone and bent pieces of 2-inch wood from stem to stern. These ribbands gave us the actual shape of the boat. During no other phase of construction would there be as much immediate change and gratification. We would later clamp the steam-bent frames to the insides of the ribbands.

(For anyone interested in the technical aspects of building a traditional wooden vessel, I recommend Bud McIntosh's 1987 book, *How to Build a Wooden Boat,* published by *WoodenBoat* magazine. The book is all you need. It is a compilation of the many articles Bud wrote for the magazine over 10 years and is superbly illustrated by Sam Manning. Hold the book in one hand and build with the other. It is easier than it looks.)

Hot steam is required for shaping the oak frames.When heated properly, they bend like spaghetti. The steam, provided by a heavy-duty boiler, was directed through a pipe and into a wooden box, where the frames were placed. Unless plenty of steam escapes from the cracks in the box, the temperature will not be hot enough to relax the fibers in the wood.

Good, white steam requires a roaring fire, and we used wood, adding pieces under the boiler every few minutes. It takes about an hour-

Doris tending the steam boiler used for bending the frames.

and-a-half to steam a 3-inch-square frame that has been split in half. Around the sharp turns, as in the transom, the 3-inch frames need to be split four times to prevent them from cracking. Timing is important, and the frames need to be bent as soon as they are removed from the steam box. Every second of delay means the wood is that much cooler and thus less flexible.

I tried to convince Doris that the wood needed to be delivered on a dead run. At this point, it was June, and we had a hot spell with temperatures in the 90s. Doris was wearing her winter coat and gloves to protect her from the steam, and by the end of the day, her pace got slower and slower and the bending harder and harder. She would hand me the hot frames and I would jam them into a socket. Then standing on the lower end of the frame, I would grab the tops and bend them into place. At the same time, Doris would clamp them to the ribbands. Once we started the transom, it became the longest 56 feet she had ever run. I soon wished I had constructed the steam box closer to the stern.

We used the 2-inch Port Orford cedar for planking and were fortunate to be able to get our good friend Paul Rollins from York, Maine, to come up and work with us for a few weeks. He had recently replanked Bill Robinson's schooner *Varua* in American Samoa.

Steam bent frames in place. Note locking stern post knee.

Doris wrote in her log:

Part of my job in helping to plank the hull was pounding in the copper spikes and holding "Dolly," a 25-pound weight with a long, pencil-shaped tip that you pressed up against the head of the nail. The person on the inside of the hull would first cut off the end of the copper nail and then peen it over with a hammer. "Dolly" could be a cruel partner, however, for her 25 pounds of iron felt like 1,000 pounds by the end of an hour. My complaint, however, was not in "Dolly's" performance but in the lack of stimulus she offered. Complaining of boredom, I was quickly put inside and asked to peen. After an hour and 200 nails, my arm was screaming to have shock absorbers installed. I quickly decided one job was as bad as the other, so was content to alternate jobs. During the planking, we worked literally from dawn to dusk and completed it in five weeks.

In September, I was committed to skippering Bill Alexander's windjammer *Timberwind*, which offers week-long charters out of Rockport, Maine. This would help keep food on the table since our project was rapidly eating up our cash. Also, Doris would have a rest after the many hours she had put in. No job was too complicated or too heavy for her. She had chiseled out half the keel and stem rabbet, driven the fastenings, and caulked the entire boat. I managed to convince her that caulking was a woman's job. For a 56-foot schooner, it is time-consuming, requiring about 1,400 hours and demanding the patience of a woman. In her log, Doris wrote:

> It was my job to caulk the hull. It is a job usually reserved for the expert boatbuilder or even a bona fide boat caulker who has spent a lifetime perfecting the art of putting that fluffy piece of cotton into seams that at best are closed in the back and slightly open in the front and at worst open on both sides. The idea is to set the cotton with a good thump of the mallet, making the two metal bands on the end sing just the right tune that tells you the cotton is set properly. On this particular boat, Herb had decided it was a woman's job. I wondered if I should have passed the news on to the men at the commercial shipyards. The statement had not been made with a lot of conviction. In fact, I remembered Herb commenting that he thought he would have a heart attack before he got the caulking on *Appledore II* done. Of course on *Appledore II*, the seams had separated and were unusually large; there was also oakum that had to be set. With *Appledore III*, the planks were dry and did not open up and we did not use oakum on top of the cotton. I had known from the start what a tough job it was, but the challenge was too good to pass up. I found there was indeed a lot to learn.
>
> The heavy lifting and pushing finally took its toll. I did not pay enough attention to how I held my back when lifting, and one spring day a pain shot down my leg and an explosion went off in my back. I stood transfixed, not daring to move a muscle. Herb had just started to head out of the boatshop for lunch. Suddenly I could not speak above a whisper and I watched with horror and disbelief as he walked up the driveway. Look back, I prayed, but he never turned around. In frustration, I dared to yell several profane words but all that came out was a gasp of pain. For 15

Planking the hull.

minutes, I stood waiting for the pain to go away. A stream of water flowed beneath my feet so the thought of lying down was out. I was finally able to take a few shuffling steps. It took me a long while, but I made it to the house. "Where have you been?" Herb asked. It did not take long to vent my pain and frustration on him. He listened calmly and rather unsympathetically remarked, "That is not going to get you out of building this boat. Forget the pain. Even if I have to carry you on a stretcher, I can't do it without you." Although I expressed irritation, inside I felt pleased that he really did need my help. Herb could do so many things well and effortlessly, and I had often found it hard working with him.

The problem was not as bad as I feared, and I soon learned to be careful and heed the warning signs.

During the winter, we kept up a steady pace from 7:00 a.m. until 6:00 p.m., every day except Sunday. When it was below zero in the morning, we tried to heat the building with a woodstove and kerosene burner, but it was not until the sun came out that we got enough heat to take off our jackets and allow the paint to dry.

Doris caulking the hull.

One night, I stood on the deck of my schooner and watched the full moon move slowly through the overhead rafters. I felt that the vessel was coming alive. I often wonder if there is not something to the relationship between our body cells and the cells of trees. They are both living cells. There is a special feeling aboard a wooden craft that one does not find in a steel or fiberglass vessel. Perhaps it could have something to do with the magnetism of the earth not being disrupted or the fact trees supply life-giving oxygen. Regardless, wood is a wonderful thing.

When Bud McIntosh was in his seventy-ninth year, after having built more than 50 vessels, I asked him what he missed most. He told me that his fondest desire was to be building wooden boats, sawing out a locust knee or planing and fitting the planking. He wished that he had the strength to continue. After building three schooners myself, I could now understand his feelings.

As time went on, we got more and more attention. Doris recalls:

It was fun to watch the reactions of people in the area. A boat project of this magnitude had never been attempted here, so the whole idea was intriguing if not downright insane. "What are you building, Noah's Ark?" "Expecting a flood in the near future?" With the record rainfall we had that spring, it might have made one pause and wonder.

It did not take long for people to learn of our boat. The building was a billboard in itself. At one time, we had planned to start a dairy farm in Littleton and a few farmers must have been chuckling about our strange new barn.

One of the best advantages was that we got to know many of our neighbors after two years — not that it was their fault that we had waited so long. Herb and I are very reclusive at times.

With our tight schedule, visitors sometimes were a problem. Often an untimely visitor would walk in when we were right in the middle of some project asking the most mundane questions like, "That's the front of the boat isn't it?" pointing to the stern. Actually, this is part of the fun of building. Talk about puffed-out chests and super egos. These Yankees, however, are a cautious lot. It took several weeks of watching our progress to ascertain whether we did in fact know what we were doing before most local people would outwardly show interest and identify us as having a worthwhile project.

One of the most-asked questions was, "Aren't you proud of your husband? This is so fantastic!" This while I was breaking my butt moving a 200-pound piece of oak. One day, my back still painful, my hand resting on the pin maul for support, I answered, "It's me he should be proud of."

We got many calls from would-be boatbuilders with a misplaced sense of the romantic; free labor just to work on a project of this kind. We knew that after two days of dull, monotonous work, the romance would be sweated away, so we never took them up on their offers.

After the boat is planked, it is about 30 percent completed. You don't see much change from then on, but there is hidden work — thousands of man-hours yet to come. It is overwhelming if you stop to think about it, so you try not to; you just keep putting in 10- or 12-hour days. With the two of us working full time, we made good progress but with only four months until launching, we were fortunate to receive the help of our friend and next- door neighbor, John Detcheverry.

(above) Doris cutting out frame sockets on horn timber. (below) The mitered transom.

John had never worked on a boat before, but he was one of the finest carpenters in the North Country. In the hectic months that followed, he did any job I asked with great speed and ease. Jobs that would take two boatbuilders on the clock in a professional shipyard two weeks to complete, John would finish by himself in a week. This proved Bud McIntosh's theory: 'A good carpenter can build a boat without any problems.' There may be a few tricks, but you can learn those from *WoodenBoat* articles, as I did. John Detcheverry was excellent for us. We only wished that we could have afforded to keep him longer.

At the same time, we hired Lucky Simino to work part-time on the grueling job of fairing and sanding the hull. A cloud of dust always followed him, but he had youth on his side. I would never forget doing that same job on *Appledore II*.

By April, the boat was 60 percent finished and was able to be transported to the sea. We had no interior, hatches, or rigging, but we had to have the boat making money for us in May or risk not owning it for very long.

One evening just before we were to move the boat, I stood under the hull looking at the turn of the bilge, the graceful curves, the fullness of the transom, and the beautiful sheerline. Again I thought of Bud. He must be a man who appreciates the graceful shapes of a woman. I returned to the house and told Doris about my thoughts. She looked at me strangely. "I have never known anyone to be turned on by a boat," she remarked jokingly. "It's just a material thing," I replied, "but its form has to rank high among the most beautiful things in the world."

With jacks and rollers we loaded *Appledore* on a flatbed trailer, taking most of one long day. At 5:00 the next morning, *Appledore*, with her gleaming, freshly painted hull, pulled away from her birthplace and started her first voyage through the White Mountains to the sea. Doris christened her with a bottle of champagne.

As *Appledore* went through New Hampshire's Franconia Notch, we stopped beneath the famous Old Man of the Mountain, a natural silhouette of an old man's profile in the granite of Cannon Mountain. The sun's rays were high enough in the east to illuminate his face. Many people and the press were following *Appledore*, and they captured the moment on film.

Our route took us toward Newburyport, Massachusetts, a site determined by bridge clearances; we needed 15 feet. It took two days to reach Newburyport, where *Appledore* was to be launched at Dick Shulman's Yankee Marine.

A few days later, we stepped the mast with a crane at the Windward Yacht Yard. Alone, I motored (with a new 52-h.p. Westerbeke engine) 120 miles down the coast to our homeport of Boothbay Harbor.

(above) Tom helping out on deck. (below) Looking aft after riveting.

We made our Memorial Day deadline, took out our first passengers, and soon we were into another summer season. Much to our delight, we had a fantastic season and were able to hire Maine carpenters John Abbe, Dave Hagan, and Paul Francy to work nights to help us complete the interior. Whenever a bunk was finished, someone quickly occupied it. We did not install the toilet or stove until the fall. Without the kindness of Jack Gibbons, the owner of Boothbay Navigation Company and manager of Fisherman's Wharf, we would not have been ready that fall for a world trip. He let us use the electric power and allowed us to set up a large tablesaw on the dock, even though it was the busy season. We were concerned about the noise we made, but Jack told us not to worry about it. He felt that some guests would actually enjoy watching our progress.

Great satisfaction comes from preparing a boat for a world voyage, especially if you have built the boat yourself. What appeals to me most is the challenge of getting all the pieces together and having the boat ready on time. There is so much to do and so little time that unless you set a departure date at the beginning, you will never get away. I find it best even to have an itinerary for the entire voyage and try to follow it fairly closely. If you don't follow the plan, the trip can easily get out of hand, and you find yourself doing such foolish things as sailing one or more oceans in hurricane or cyclone season.

As we had discovered in the past, finding the right crew members is not an easy task. Looking for enthusiasm and commitment rather than experience, we started by letting the word out that we were departing on a certain date, by advertising in Yankee and Sail magazines, and by printing the information in our summer brochures. The initial response was good. Some of the applicants were genuinely interested, but most were not. We always get some unusual requests. Before this trip, a woman called and asked if she could bring her two dogs. I told her she would have to contribute the same amount for each dog, since they would occupy the same amount of space as any crew member would. I doubt she had an accurate picture of Appledore's size when she made the request. Needless to say, she changed her mind.

We never presented our voyages as romantic fantasy. Instead, we tried to deal with facts, but, generally, once people are hooked, nothing will change their minds. Many times, despite our discussions, people saw only the romantic side, blinding themselves to the hardships we described. It would be to our disadvantage later in the trip when reality finally sank in and people became disillusioned, although I have always admired the courage of the few who decided to join us and face an unknown experience.

Appledore III *crossing the Merrimack River at Newburyport.*

On this voyage, we planned to leave with only five crew members. At the beginning, we could afford to leave one berth open because we would be shooting a film and getting a small salary and expenses.

A frenzy of activity marked the last four weeks before our departure. We worked well into each night storing supplies and spare parts. Sample's shipyard gave us a complimentary haul out to paint the bottom; an old fashion bon voyage gesture. Barry Johnston, the chief cook at Fisherman's Wharf, was extremely helpful. He let us order everything wholesale through Fisherman's Wharf and went out of his way to get us everything we needed. Each night, after our interior cabinetwork was secured, we loaded the contents of more than 300 cases of food into every conceivable space. By now, at least, Tommy and Lisa had bunks. We also had rigging work and new installations to finish. The days were so hectic and confusing that I had to write myself notes on what I needed to get done the next day.

A week before departure, our crew began arriving. Twenty-one-year-old Bob Royal, a local lobsterman, had been the first to sign up, but he had just gotten into a serious car accident and would not be joining us until we reached Rio. We were now down to four crew members. Ray Corbett, 61, was a retired railroad company auditor from Connecticut. He had told us that this trip was something he would really enjoy, and he

(above) Appledore III *at Fisherman's Wharf, two days before departure.*
(below) Doris, Bob Royal, Chris Merriam, Ray Corbett and Day Allen. Kate Harris missing from picture. Boutilier photo.

hoped we would not turn him down because of age. On our previous world voyage, I had taken couples in their sixties and they had worked out well. I did not hesitate, therefore, to take Ray. He was also a part-time lobsterman and was in good shape. We did believe, however, that young people had the advantage on this particular trip. It would not be easy sailing through the Strait of Magellan and around the Cape of Good Hope.

We had also decided on Day Allen, 18, who had just graduated from high school in Portland, Oregon. Chris Merriam, 20, from Bowling Green, Ohio, had been attending the University of Southern Maine in Portland. Kate Harris, 19, from Newcastle, Maine, was a sophomore at Dartmouth College. For Tommy, our eight-year-old son, it would be his second voyage around the world, and for Lisa, his three-year-old sister, it would be her first.

A foggy departure for the world voyage. Appledore *is heavily laden with five tons of supplies. Boutilier photo.*

Outward Bound: Maine to Brazil

November 5 was a rainy, foggy day. A light southerly breeze was blowing into Boothbay Harbor, but it failed to dampen our excitement. We would depart at 2:00 p.m. as planned. Friends were gathering to wish us farewell.

In her log, Doris wrote:

> All morning, the carpenters were madly dashing around trying to get last-minute things done, a replay of *Appledore II* and our first world trip. Wires were strung everywhere like spider webs. Any ordinary person would have concluded that at 2:00 p.m., we would not be sailing, but I had witnessed the miracle of departure day before.
>
> I had one last thing to buy that morning. Tommy had had a couple of mishaps the last few days, losing two pairs of shoes overboard. He even had to attend a farewell party in his stocking feet. Threatening dire consequences should anything happen to either shoe, we bought yet another pair of shoes at a local store.
>
> Bob Royal, our injured crewman, hobbled about on crutches, very disappointed that he could not leave with us. Considering it had only been a week since he had broken his leg in three places and had it pinned, I thought it miraculous that he should be standing with the rest of us in the group pictures.
>
> Many thoughtful people were handing us packages of cookies, cakes, and jams. The day before, we had received a wreath of flowers from Mr. Wilder, a Boothbay native.
>
> As we waited for the lines to be thrown off, Tommy held the wreath that he would throw into the harbor, a quaint custom designed to ensure our safe return. His second-grade teacher brought him notes of farewell from his class and a gold pin on a

card telling him he was the star of his second-grade class. Lisa's daycare lady gave her a huge card of farewell, telling her they would miss her. Lisa was oblivious to what was happening. While the rest of us rushed around, she contentedly washed her toy dishes in the forward cabin.

At 2:00 p.m., we cast off our docklines and got underway. A few yards from the dock, we hoisted full sail and Tommy tossed the wreath of flowers off the stern. We eased the sheets and headed out to sea. The voyage had officially begun.

The flower wreath floated slowly across the harbor toward Fisherman's Wharf. It was a final farewell. Some local boats carrying friends and relatives followed us out, but once in the outer harbor, we were slowly enveloped by thick fog.

Doris and I had been up late every night the previous few weeks, and I did not look forward to being up all night navigating against the wind down the fogbound coast. The weatherman was calling for northerly winds in the morning, so I decided to call at Southport Island and lay alongside Eliot Winslow's tug *Charles Winslow*, for the evening. Captain Jeff Lozier invited us to use their fresh water and the galley on board so we could conserve our 160-gallon supply, which was supposed to last us until Brazil. For the first time that evening, we sat together around the cherry table in the main cabin and had a quiet dinner.

In the morning, the weather had vastly improved. The sky was clear and a light northerly breeze blew; we were off at dawn. Captain Campbell on the *Balmy Days* called to wish us good luck. He said he would be waiting for us in 18 months, which was encouraging. He had faith we would return.

Off Portland, Maine, the fishing boat *Carrie* came alongside. The captain threw us a 12-pound cod and a 2-pound lobster, which improved our outlook for dinner.

Tommy and Lisa had been unusually quiet all day. They were exhausted from all the commotion during the previous few weeks. Listening to a radio broadcast, we heard that Ronald Reagan had beaten Walter Mondale by a landslide and would be our president for the next four years. There was not much celebration on board, since it had been a foregone conclusion. Knowing we would be underway on election day, most of us had voted by absentee ballot.

At 10:00 p.m., the wind was picking up from the north and we reefed the mainsail. Our course was to take us around Cape Ann. Once there, I would decide if we would go outside of Cape Cod or inside through the canal. The seas were building, but we had no complaints, since it was a perfect wind for sailing south. Just before dawn, a whale surfaced not more than 15 feet away. It matched the speed of *Appledore* precisely. Seeing the huge black body in the full moonlight reminded me of the accounts I had read about whales sinking boats, although I doubt they do it intentionally. He disappeared for a moment and must have gone right under the hull, for he resurfaced on the other side not more than 10 feet away. I could smell his bad breath. He spouted several more times, then dropped back and followed in our wake for five minutes. I thought to myself, there must be a lot of divine guidance in sailing safely around the world in a small wooden boat.

By morning, the wind was blowing 30 knots and the seas were building to 8 feet. Some of our gear was not secured as well as it could have been. Camera equipment was still strewn all over the aft cabin floor and onions, potatoes, and squash strained to escape from their mesh bags. The Cape Cod Canal was only a three-hour broad reach away, so I chose that course.

As we were entering the canal, our VHF radio began reporting a hurricane making up off the Puerto Rican coast. Although it was a long way away, it was something to be concerned about. We have always departed from New England as late as possible in the fall to avoid the hurricane season, and now we had one directly in our path.

It was with some reluctance that, after coming out of Buzzards Bay, we pointed the bow toward Bermuda. Looking at the situation carefully, I saw that the eastern half of the United States was in a high-pressure cell, which was moving off the East Coast. It seemed unlikely that Hurricane Claus would head east, and, as we listened to more reports, the hurricane did not seem to be going anywhere. With the 20-knot north wind, we would be off Bermuda in four days, and if the hurricane started to move north, we would be able to duck in there.

We all had to adjust to the motion of a ship at sea. This part of a long ocean passage requires the most effort. The seas were soon up to 15 feet, and the motion of *Appledore* sailing from crest to crest certainly was nothing like a daysail along the Maine coast. It was amazing how well everyone did. In two days, we were serving huge meals. Even Hampie, our year-old hamster, seemed to be doing well. All night long, we listened to the squeak of his exercise wheel as he ran nonstop.

A northeast wind brought warmer temperatures as we entered the Gulf Stream. A large swell setting in from the east, combined with a northerly wind blowing against the current, made things quite sloppy. One wave caught us broadside and broke over the forward cabin, with spray going over the mainmast.

At daybreak on November 10, we were definitely in tropical waters. Although the winds had moderated from the northeast, we still had 5- to 10-foot swells. As I sat behind the wheel, we had a private showing of a beautiful sunrise. The water was turquoise blue, speckled with bits of floating sargasso weed. Porpoises swam playfully in front of the bow. Tommy's and Lisa's eyes were as big as half dollars as they watched these mammals leap out of the water beside the boat.

When the wind went behind us, the crew struggled at the wheel. Downwind steering is always difficult for new helmsmen. There is more to being a good helmsman than one might imagine. It is a subconscious thing. You feel a change in the roll and pitch, which you compensate for with the appropriate rudder. You feel the wind at your face or in your hair and you know when you are off course. Some people never get it. I questioned whether I would have been better off investing my money in a self-steerer than in the wind generator that sat in the counter, unusable because the factory forgot to send an essential part. The sails and rigging, however, were new, and they could take a little abuse while everyone got used to the wheel.

I soon found we would have to learn the new teenage lingo if our relationship was to be "the balls," which means great. When I went down for dinner, our cook of the day asked me if I would like my hamburger "raw," without the roll. The burger was "awesome." I could understand the words, but when it came to using "far out," "tense," and "intense," I finally gave up. It was too "radical" for me.

Halfway to Bermuda, I made a routine check of the bilges and to my surprise found a lot of water. We pumped it out, but it immediately started filling up again. Finally I traced the problem to the rudder stuffing box, which I had neglected to pack with flax. When new, it was tight enough and in Boothbay Harbor we never pitched enough to put the stuffing box below the waterline, so no water had ever come through it. At sea, with the pitching and rolling, the stuffing box was below the surface of the water half of the time. At 2:00 a.m., I unpacked the counter and crawled in to pack the stuffing box. With no light except a flashlight, and with the ship rolling, it was not easy, but that took care of the leak. Now that I no longer heard water sloshing in the bilges, I slept well. Thanks to Doris's good caulking job, this boat was completely dry.

On Monday, November 12, four-and-a-half days after we left the East Coast, we were sailing into the lovely harbor of Saint George, Bermuda. The only telltale sign of the hurricane was a large swell from the east. Yet at the moment it was still directly in our path for going further south.

Tom in Galapagos, first voyage.

We spent five days in Bermuda, using most of that time to secure the boat for our next long passage to Brazil. We put up a net around the lifelines to help keep the kids on board. The net was made from twine used for parlor heads in lobster traps, and since Doris had once earned extra money making these for a lobsterman, she created a nice arrangement of 3-foot-high netting around the whole boat.

During our second day in port, we were hit by a strong gale, with 40-knot winds from the southwest. So much sand blew on board that we lost sight of the deck. Several yachts were caught out at sea and sustained damage but were able to make it into port. Many yachtsmen heading for Bermuda from the United States fail to realize how rough the passage can be, and often they are not prepared. I have never sailed to Bermuda in October or November without getting into some bad weather. The North Atlantic requires a lot of respect, especially around the Gulf Stream.

We hoped to reach Recife, Brazil, on December 3, and then Rio for Christmas. On our first world trip we had taken the more conventional route to the Pacific through the Panama Canal, but on this trip I wanted

Catching fish.
Tom and Herb,
Chris and Bob.

to see the Strait of Magellan. I had long been fascinated by accounts about Ferdinand Magellan, the man who engineered the first circumnavigation of the globe, and it was exciting to think of seeing places that Magellan had seen centuries earlier. I was also being drawn back to the desolation of the Antarctic where I had spent a couple of years of my life.

On November 17, a rain squall came through as we departed Bermuda. On the gust of wind that it generated, we were carried out to sea and toward Brazil. Hurricane Claus had cleared out and posed no threat. For the next 500 miles, the wind was either too light or from the wrong direction, and we used 60 gallons of fuel trying to make southward progress. Since we only carried about 200 gallons, this was a serious problem. We still had 3,000 miles to go to reach Brazil.

We finally picked up the tradewinds at 19 degrees north, but they were from the southeast, putting us on a port tack headed for Trinidad. We kept this tack for a few days, and whenever the wind backed to the east, we would steer closer to Brazil. We were fortunate that *Appledore* could sail close to the wind.

In December, the wind was supposed to blow from the east and northeast, but we were encountering a steady breeze from the southeast. At one point I looked through my inventory of charts to see if I had any for a landfall along the coast of Guyana (formerly British Guiana).

During this period, Tommy did some fishing and caught four large fish. We ate the two mahimahi and released two others, a 60-pound wahoo and an 80-pound marlin. It was the best fishing that we ever experienced. We also began to see more flying fish than ever before, and one night 11 of them landed on board. One hit Chris at the helm and another landed on Kate after bouncing off the sail. This can give you a terrible fright on a dark night. These "flying fish" cannot actually fly, but they have wings and soar over the surface of the water at about five feet to escape the larger fish that feed on them. On our first world trip, we had had two cats that considered them a great delicacy. Even when the cats slept down below, they were sensitive to the peculiar thud that meant a fish had hit the deck. One of the cats had the habit of bringing her catch to our cabin so that she could eat and enjoy it leisurely. In the morning we would find the floor and deck littered with wings, the only part of the fish the cats would not eat.

After a few days at sea, you stop noticing the motion of the boat and begin to establish a rhythm and a routine, taking each day as it comes. You never need to look at a clock unless you are relieving the watch. The height of the sun determines the time. At dawn, it is cool and invigorating, but as the sun emerges and the air begins to warm up, the pace slows. At noon, you seek shade, trying to move as little as possible.

Crossing the Equator: Chris, Day, Tom, Kate and Doris.

Lisa and Day.

Only in late afternoon can you stand unprotected from the sun's rays, and then people slowly begin to come to life. For me, dusk is the best time. There is the evening meal, a sunset, the first twinkling stars, and, best of all, cool air. Life is centered on steering, eating, and sleeping.

A new item aboard on this voyage was the satellite navigator (Sat-Nav for short). It would give us our position every couple of hours, and as long as it continued to work, things were much easier for me. I used my extra time for filming scenes on board or catching up with my correspondence. Some argue that the satellite navigator takes something away from the challenge of sailing around the world, but I disagree. The navigational tables and nautical almanac used for celestial navigation are prepared by the same computer that the Sat-Nav uses, so great technology has been applied in both methods. In the old days, when the navigator had to figure the astronomical triangles himself, he required some skill.

One of the biggest morale boosters was turning on the refrigerator. When the engine was running, we were able to chill beverages or even make Jell-O and cheesecake. When we were strictly sailing, we did not have the electric power to operate the refrigerator for very long, since it would quickly drain our four industrial 12-volt batteries. Before leaving a port, we tried to stock the 50-pound refrigerator full of fresh meat and chicken, depending on what was available. We generally set it on freeze, figuring that once the meat was frozen, it would take less power to keep the refrigerator going. After that supply was exhausted, we would have canned food. Among our choices were Swanson boneless chicken, beef stew, tuna, salmon, Danish ham, corned beef, and LaChoy products. Occasionally we had fresh fish, and always potatoes, canned vegetables, and as many fresh vegetables as we could keep in the heat of the cabins. Desserts were limited only by the imaginations of the cooks. Although we ate well, there was always a yearning to get into port for something new. Our mouths would water at the thought of a hamburger and cold Coke, and discussions often were dominated by the talk of the next restaurant and bar.

Doris was in charge of the galley, but she left it loose. Her only guidelines were to indicate the meat and vegetable for the day. The cook prepared it any way he or she saw fit. We each cooked one day and had as many days off as there were other people on board. I was fortunate to have Doris with me. Since I do not like to cook and she does not like to steer, we swapped duties. Everyone prepared his or her own breakfast, because several of the crew, especially the women who had the 12:00 to 4:00 watch, ate little in the morning. I often wondered if it was not self-preservation. Once the men got up, the going got pretty rough in the galley. There is no such thing as chivalry when it comes to filling a man's empty stomach.

It was interesting to watch the different styles of preparation. Day Allen bustled about, getting it done as quickly as possible with the least fuss, and when the meal was ready, she slung it bartender-style across the table. Ray told us how much cooking did not bother him. No one got near his galley. Chris was laid back; goulash with hamburger, rice and cabbage; help-yourself-it's-ready. Kate was more professional and efficient. When Doris was in the mood, she was elaborate. Bob was "potluck," needing a day of free advice and a dozen hands in the stew, but it always seemed to come out fine.

With young people on board, appetites were finicky. At every meal, there was at least one person who had an aversion to what was being served. I wondered how some would survive, but I was not about to throw everything overboard and restock in Brazil. My own particular downfall was fish. In time, we all learned to tolerate most foods, with the exception of the clam chowder. I cannot imagine what I was thinking about on the day I insisted that Doris order 13 cases of the product. We had enough on board to eat it for lunch every day of the trip, but by the end of the first case, no one could face it. Just the smell of it was enough to drive some of the crew on deck for air. By the end of the trip, I was the only one eating it, and, believe it or not, enjoying it. In Martinique, we gave several cans to the crew of another yacht. I smiled with satisfaction when we saw them again and they told us they were keeping it for when they had special company.

The same thing would happen to any food we had on board. We quickly became bored with food we all had previously enjoyed on land. With little else to do at sea, too much emphasis was put on mealtimes. We could strive for variety, but cooking at sea was not something many people enjoyed. The motion of the boat alone was enough to make you want to get it over with in the least amount of effort and time.

We carried 160 gallons of water in eight separate containers or tanks — just in case one sprung a leak or became contaminated. Since we used the water only for drinking and cooking, we had enough to last about 50 days.

As we approached the Brazilian coast, we were just short of making it around the northeast tip by 200 miles. The wind was southeast at 25 knots and we used the engine with our remaining supply of diesel fuel to reach a port called Fortaleza. It was just 25 days after our departure from Bermuda.

On arrival in Fortaleza, I took a taxicab into town to find the immigration department. Exchanging United States dollars was not a problem, since everyone was anxious to get them. With a pocket full of cruzeiros, I paid off the taxicab driver and walked a few blocks until I found the police station. Communication was difficult. Few people spoke English in this port, and I knew no Portuguese.

I was directed into a room that had a chair, a broken desk, and a telephone on the floor that was attached to a mass of tangled wires. I kept hearing, "Visa, visa!" but I didn't have one. I had checked it out with authorities in the States and was told we would be issued visas on arrival. That, apparently, was not the case. They sent for an interpreter, who informed me that I was in big trouble.

Through the interpreter I learned that I could be fined several thousand cruzeiros. Then I told them my tale of woes. I had not planned to come to Fortaleza, but we were running out of diesel fuel and needed supplies. We were on our way to the South Pacific, and Brazil had a very long coast. They accepted that story simply because they wanted to, and apparently decided not to give us a hard time. They allowed us to stay for two days to resupply. In her log, Doris wrote:

> At the yacht club, we met an English couple who had just sailed their 81-year-old yacht *Curlew* from the Azores to Fortaleza. The wife was a middle-aged dynamo clad in a blue bikini and railroad hat. Since we spoke no Portuguese, she offered to give us advice on changing our money, finding a grocery store, etc. She introduced us to the black market, Brazil's answer to failing banks. There we got a much better exchange rate. It was hard to believe that four years before, the exchange had been 150 cruzeiros per dollar. Now we were getting about 3,500 cruzeiros per dollar. The young racketeer who came to the yacht club to change our money might have come out of a mobster film. He was clad in a black suit with skin-tight pants, and the front of his shirt was left unbuttoned so the hairs on this chest were visible. The outfit was completed with a pair of highly polished black pointed shoes.
>
> We were all overjoyed to be in port again. It had been a long, hard passage. We found it a thrill just to be able to walk as far and as long as we wanted. Food and clothing were incredibly cheap, and the Jumbo Supermarket was unlike any we had seen in the States.

We took on diesel fuel and water and enjoyed anchoring next to the Brazilian sail fishing fleet. Their small boats, called *jangadas*, consist basically of a raft, a sail, and a steering oar. Two or three men roll them off the beach early each morning, using palm logs as rollers, and they sail at 5 to 6 knots out to their fishing grounds. In the late afternoon, they begin coming back to sell their catch. There were about 100 of them, all with different-colored sails and commercial designs. The fishermen here have used this design for 400 years. The modern high-rises of the city formed the backdrop, making for an interesting contrast between the new and the old.

Jangadas, *fishing boats at Fortaleza.*

After two days in Fortaleza, we departed, and the wind came out of the northeast, making it possible to sail directly around the northeast tip of Brazil and on to Recife on the east coast in five days.

One afternoon, as we were coming around the bulge of Brazil, we were visited by an Air Force jet. He was not satisfied with one pass but came by several times, flying at lower and lower altitudes until he was about mast height. We could see the pilot clearly in the cockpit. On his final run, he dipped his wings and waved. Later in the afternoon, the jet returned, this time with a friend. They did a couple of passes but did not show off to quite the extent that our lone visitor had done earlier.

Now that the winds were light and the seas calm, Doris was able to get a school schedule established. She recalls:

> Tommy would miss two years of public school by going on this trip. Most of the cruising people we had known had used the Calvert Correspondence program out of Baltimore, Maryland, and had good success, so we decided to use their program. Tommy had started second grade in Boothbay Harbor before he left and had been doing very well — so well, in fact, that his teacher suggested I skip second grade and go into third. Never having taught school before, I did not feel comfortable enough to do that.

Doris and the children making Cabbage Patch dolls.

I needed second grade more than Tommy. After we had finished the second- grade work, however, and gone on to the third, I realized that her suggestion had been an excellent one.

Sailing conditions were having more of an effect on our classes than I had expected. Neither of us wanted to study when it was rough, and in port, there was so much to see and do and so little time to do it in, that port days became a holiday. I felt Tommy got more of an education on shore than he did with his nose stuck in a book. I began to worry, however, that we would never finish the program. To compensate, we would do two or three lessons together. I found that grouping lessons still took us less than three hours a day, and that was more stimulating for him.

The course was well laid out, with instructions designed for a teacher who had had no training. I was pleased with the subject matter. Tommy and I looked forward to the reading segment, which often combined reading with interesting stories about historical figures. We visited some of the places where several of these had gained fame, making his lessons and our port visits more meaningful. This was also the earliest I had ever seen mythology taught, and it became a favorite part of the lesson. By this time, Tommy was reading enough extra material that he was often coming upon examples of its use in literature today.

Math was our main source of trouble — not because he had difficulty learning it but because he hated to practice his tables. For Tommy, it was drudgery, and it became our battleground. The first couple of weeks, it had taken us well over an hour to go over the flash cards. I pulled my hair in despair until one day there was something he wanted to do in the worst way. That day, it took us less than two minutes to go through the hundred or so cards. The secret was out of the bag, and math became less grueling for both of us.

He would do 20 lessons and then take a test, which would be sent to a teacher in Baltimore who would correct it and give suggestions on what and how to improve in certain areas. I found I had to guard myself from helping too much on the tests. It's a natural instinct to want to see your child do a perfect job. You might not offer him the answers, but the stress you add by demanding perfection can be just as damaging.

I had worried that I was slowing Tommy down, but when he returned to public school and took the California achievement tests that all fourth-graders were taking, he came out in the 98th percentile. I breathed a sigh of relief and happily retired my chalk and blackboard.

I would not hesitate to teach Tommy again, but I felt that for a while he needed to be back in a school system again. We would not always live in the fairy-tale world of *Appledore*.

In Recife, our problems with immigration were even worse than in Fortaleza. We called the American consulate, but they could offer little assistance. With the help of Brian Stevens, an Englishman we met at the yacht club, I took a taxi to the immigration office, where I didn't get a very warm welcome. "You've entered illegally and we are going to do what they should have done in Fortaleza, fine you and impound your boat."

After their initial tough stance, the man in charge went on to explain that a friend of his had gone by plane to the United States without a visa and the American authorities had refused to let him off the plane.

Finally, they worked it out that we could stay three or four days to take on fuel and water, and on Christmas Day no one would be around to clear us. Then we would have 48 hours to clear.

In an attempt to help us, an influential member of the yacht club told us things we could do in order to be allowed to stay. As he explained it, the law is the law, but in Brazil there are always ways to make it work for you. If we had something to repair on the boat, we could get permission to stay. They warned us, however, not to claim anything too major. If the authorities thought you were unseaworthy they would not allow you to leave until they were satisfied. Second, if anyone was sick, they would not force us to leave. "Doctors are very important people in Brazil. If they would write a note to the authorities saying someone needed to stay for treatment, the authorities would not refuse."

Recife is a commercial shipping port with an unusual blend of new and old, rich and poor. We were made very welcome at the Recife Yacht Club and were allowed to use their showers, bar, and restaurant. At the same time, our hull was being cleaned by thousands of green crabs and little silver fish that fed on the algae. When we were below decks, we could hear them pecking at the bottom.

Despite our visa problems, we spent Christmas anchored 50 yards off the yacht club, where Christmas lights were strung up, creating a nice holiday atmosphere. We decorated the boat with ornaments we had brought from Maine. Doris and the kids made fudge and gingerbread men and we were able to do our Christmas shopping in downtown stores. The selections were not great, but they were adequate.

We took the opportunity to visit the Casa de Cultura, a former prison that had been converted into a craft market. Each of the prison cells on the three levels contained separate shops. The crafts included mahogany plaques, hand-sewn linen clothing, leatherwork, and canvas and clay dolls. Members of the yacht club had suggested that we be sure to take advantage of the incredibly low prices here. "People farther south," they explained, "know the value of art." Doris was happy. She gets no greater pleasure on these trips than to pound the pavement looking for inexpensive crafts.

I am sure if you asked anyone in the *Appledore* crew whether they liked Recife, the answer would be yes. We did meet many other people, however, who had stopped there and had nothing good to say about it. Unfortunately, the club is located on the far side of a slum area, and we were warned not to walk through there at night. To get a taxi, however, it was often necessary to do so. We never had any problem, probably because we were obviously American tourists.

On December 27, we sailed from Recife for Rio. It was a routine passage downwind with one exception: a thunder-and-lightning storm with a tornado halfway to Rio. It changed the routine radically.

At 2:00 a.m. on January 3, Day Allen was on watch. The sky had become black and *Appledore* began to heel under an increasing wind. I went up on deck to check things out, and suddenly a blast of wind and rain struck the schooner and heeled her over, burying the starboard side of the vessel under four feet of water. To ease the pressure on the sails, we either had to get some sail down or head the boat up into the wind, but at that moment, we could do neither, because we had lost all headway.

Majestic Christ statue, with 92 foot arm spread, Rio.

Our watertight Bomar hatches were all dogged down, and Doris had quickly put in the splashboards in the main companionway, so there was little chance of water getting below. Instead of falling off to gain speed, I turned on the engine to full power to bring the bow up closer to the wind, which eased the heel. We began to pick up speed. I thought for a moment that this blast of strong wind (known by Brazilians as a tornado, but not to be confused with our midwestern killer tornadoes) would subside almost immediately, but that was not to be. The wind remained steady at 40 knots, and we had to lower the foresail for a few hours. At dawn, the wind dropped to almost calm, and we used the engine. All day, we made only 4 knots toward the south, and by dusk, although we could still see lightning behind us, the stars were out ahead.

Our arrival in Rio was a bit of a letdown. To our surprise, it was foggy, so we couldn't see much as we sailed into what is reputed to be one of the prettiest harbors in the world. We had no idea where to tie up or anchor in such a large harbor, so we tried unsuccessfully to call on our VHF radio. No one spoke English. As we were taking down our sails, a Brazilian yacht sailed across the harbor and came alongside. They gave us advice on where to go, and we soon found ourselves anchored with other foreign yachts in a smooth, protected basin at the municipal marina.

It was a bit spooky at first. There were armed guards all around the perimeter of the marina. I counted 10 on duty. Later, I casually inquired about the security and was told we were in a high-crime area and there would be "much thievery without the security guards." Rio, "River of January," is like every big city in that respect. We were warned to be careful, and the women were often reminded to take off their jewelry, no matter how inexpensive it was. We had no trouble, however, and found the Brazilians to be extremely compassionate and friendly. Two of our crew members, Kate and Day, were welcomed into the home of a Brazilian couple during our stay in Rio.

In Rio, I tackled the visa requirement differently. I went to the authorities and asked, "Can I get permission for one of our crew members to see a doctor? We are on our way south to the Strait of Magellan to gain access to the South Pacific and need to make an emergency call for medical help." Permission was granted. Doris in fact had an infected ear, and I took her to an ear specialist the American Embassy had recommended. After cleaning it out and prescribing antibiotics, the doctor wrote a letter to the authorities stating that she would need to return in 10 days. Thus, we were granted a 10-day visa. It was only because of their good nature that we were permitted to stay. I still had to spend three days in the Federal Police building while the men in charge argued about how to fill out the forms. At the end of that time, they took a mug shot, fingerprinted all of us, and finally stamped temporary visas in our passports.

In Rio Harbor, the captain of a posh American yacht tied up to the marina wall invited us all to a cocktail party. A paid crew maintained the 70-foot vessel and was preparing her for a visit by the owners. The wall-to-wall carpet was taken up, the cushions removed, and the brasswork wrapped in plastic. Lisa eyed the pink panther on the pillow of a large double bed but thankfully made no attempt to snatch it. It was interesting to see the luxurious way some people sail. I still preferred *Appledore*.

Rio Harbor is unusual and scenic. A hundred or more ships were anchored or tied up. Inside the harbor, pitons rise straight up out of the water and the tops are so high that often they are in clouds. Unlike New York and Miami, Rio's tall buildings seem to blend in majestically. They never quite catch the tips of the mountain peaks behind them. A cable car to the top of Sugarloaf Mountain provides a grand view of Rio Harbor, but perhaps the most-visited attraction is the statue of Christ high on a hill overlooking the city. At night, we could gaze up from the deck of *Appledore* and see clouds billowing around the 124-foot-high lighted figure — looking almost as if it were suspended in the sky. The statue's hands extend out to both sides with a span of 92 feet.

Sunset, off Uruguay.

South of Rio

It is 2,300 miles from Rio to Punta Arenas, Chile, and we expected rough weather along the way — if not an easterly gale, then a southwest blow. Wind speeds can exceed 80 knots, so we spent 10 days in Rio preparing *Appledore* for such conditions. Instead of flying our regular jib, we chained on our smallest storm jib and put extra lines on everything secured on deck. We also carried an additional 110 gallons of diesel fuel in jerry cans stowed inside the skiff and a 55-gallon drum lashed on deck. This fuel was a bonus when we entered the Strait of Magellan.

On January 16, we saw the coast of Brazil for the last time. That evening, it dropped below the horizon as we sailed away to the south. We had a fair easterly breeze and all sails were set and drawing. I had hoped for just such a wind, and with the Brazilian current, we were making excellent time.

In the morning, we were 90 miles off the coast under the familiar puffy, white, tradewind clouds, and, although the wind occasionally went light, it always came back. We could still take seawater baths on deck since the water temperature had not dropped drastically.

After five days of beautiful sailing, the wind backed to the northeast and was so light that we turned on our iron wind, the 52-h.p. Westerbeke diesel engine with 2.5-to-1 reduction gear. This engine was by no means overpowering our 28-ton schooner. On the contrary, a vessel of this size could use a 180-h.p. engine. Yet, when the wind is light or there is no breeze, we can make 4 knots on a diesel consumption of only a half gallon per hour. During spells of light wind, we used the engine 24 hours a day.

Soon we were off the coast of Uruguay and approaching the Rio de la Plata area. The sky looked threatening. For the next 12 hours, the swell increased from the south and the wind picked up to 35 knots from the southeast, 45 degrees contrary to the swell. With a couple of reefs in the sails, we continued on our course, pitching over 10-foot seas.

In Rio's main square.

Within a day, the wind backed again to the northeast and dropped off. We were back to using the engine, consuming a good portion of our diesel fuel, but Mar del Plata, Argentina, reputed to be a good port of call, was only 45 miles away. A female crew member was having a medical problem, and even though it was under control with pills we had on board, we felt she should be checked out in port. Our medical kit had been put together for us by Doctor André Benoit of Boothbay Harbor. He had done some offshore cruising himself, thus it included every possible remedy imaginable. It was a good kit.

In recent days the ocean had changed from royal blue to olive green, reminding us of home. It was cold, although not yet the temperature of Maine water, but every day brought us closer to that.

Wandering albatross, open ocean companion.

We saw our first magnificent albatross. It scarcely moved its wings, which spanned 7 to 8 feet, as it glided and dipped over the swells. When the wind was light, we would see these birds sitting on the water's surface, awaiting a strong wind for a free ride. They need 30 knots of it to maintain effortless flight. For takeoff, they would literally run across the water, with their large webbed feet slapping the surface like paddle wheels.

On January 26, we arrived in Mar del Plata, where we tried anchoring in the outer harbor, but the anchor wouldn't hold. As I motored around looking for another spot, the yacht club president came out in his launch and invited us to tie up to the club floats. Fortunately, it was high tide, and we were able to make it through the narrow cut and under the raised footbridge to a small, protected basin. The yacht club did everything it could to make us welcome: free dockage, showers, and even an excellent Argentine beef barbecue at a neighboring club. This was Vito Dumas's (First Argentinian solo sailor) club and home port. One of his last boats, *Sirio* was moored close to us. On both days that we were there, people came down to the boat to chat, admire *Appledore,* and offer assistance. Here we met many people who spoke some English, which made our stay even more enjoyable than in Brazil.

The second evening, we took Tommy and Lisa to a three-ring Mexican circus being performed across the street. It was the best circus any of us had ever seen.

We still had 1,200 miles to go to Punta Arenas, and we wanted to be there in their summer season, so we thanked our Argentine hosts and pushed on. Each day that we made progress southward was a blessing, since the weather systems in this region change almost hourly. At one moment, it was completely overcast, then completely clear. The sea and air temperatures were dropping daily, and after three days, the air was down to 54°F. Tommy's hamster also must have noticed the declining temperature, because he got out of his cage and disappeared — until one of the boys nearly stepped on him.

We were concerned about the southwest fronts. The president of the Mar del Plata yacht club had told us to watch for cigar-shaped clouds. "When you see them," he said, "you can expect a full gale." Doris thought every cloud looked cigar-shaped, so she was always predicting the worst.

For a while, our wind was from the east at 12 knots, and we could sail. Six hundred miles south of Mar del Plata, a brief calm was followed by a 35-knot southwest wind dead against us. A very steep sea came up quickly. We had to tack, and since we were 40 miles off the coast, I chose to head toward shore. Once we were within four miles of the coast, the wind veered to the south and the seas calmed. We were able to motorsail and make good progress.

We did not have to wait long for a dead calm under a cloudless sky. We were 400 miles from the entrance to the Strait of Magellan. Along the coast was an unbroken line of sand dunes and cliffs. Under the 200-foot cliffs were narrow beaches that probably would be covered with water at high tide. We kept expecting to see someone appear on a beach and wave to us, but there was no sign of life: no smoke, no antennas, nothing. It was eerie. At night, a light breeze would come from the southwest over the Argentine plains and we would slide offshore. The next morning, it would back to the south and become onshore, and we would tack back in. As we got closer to the coast, our course would become more parallel, and we would make good time with motor and sails until dusk. The current also runs along the coast, but it is not excessive. It runs in both directions, so it would cancel out any negative effect on our progress. For two days, we had some peaceful motorsailing and narrowed the distance to the Strait of Magellan.

On February 6, we had just 75 miles to go to Cape Virgenes, marking the entrance to the Strait, when the barometer started a steady drop. We pushed ahead with the engine, and at dusk it was dead calm. The sun set behind the Argentine coast and a full, white moon rose over the Atlantic in a crisp, cloudless sky. This was an extra bonus, giving us plenty of illumination along the coast. Just before dark, we picked up the flash of the lighthouse on the Cape of Eleven Thousand Virgins, so named

Under fair skies, South Atlantic.

by Magellan. By now, the engine was running on diesel fumes. At midnight, we passed the lighthouse high on the cliffs overlooking Cape Virgenes, and the full moon bathed the water with so much light that we were able to take an inshore route between two rocks. One rock was just off the cape and the other, the half-submerged Nassan Rock, was 2-1/2 miles off the cape. This would save us time, since the only other choice was to give the cape a very wide berth.

A large swell came rolling in from the east. It crashed on the cliffs and probably also on Nassan Rock, but we were not close enough to the latter to find out. Ahead was Dungeness Light, marking the inner entrance to the Strait. At 1:00 a.m. on February 7, it was cold on deck, yet Tommy was taking a keen interest in our progress and was determined to stay up. The wind came out of the southwest, but it was not very strong. Once we were in the Strait, we would have some protection from the swells. After giving the watch a course that I thought would clear Dungeness Point, I went below briefly to warm up and check the charts. The lookout also went below to warm up. Soon Tommy was calling me, "Dad, you better come up here because we are getting close to shore."

I knew our course would be close, but since the water was deep right up to the shoreline, I didn't think much about it. "In a minute," I told him. "You better come up right now, Dad," he insisted. "There is something sticking out of the water ahead of us." I wondered what he was talking about, but I wasted no time getting up on deck. Sure enough, we would have been aground in another 10 minutes.

Close by was a long, dark pier jutting out from shore off our starboard bow. We had been set down onto the coast at quite a fast rate. I changed the course as Tommy asked, "Aren't you glad I called, Dad?" I replied, "I sure am, Tommy. I'm really proud of you. You're going to make a good seaman." It was 2:00 a.m. and cold, but Tommy definitely was not going below now, because he knew we needed him. We soon passed Dungeness Light and entered the Strait of Magellan.

That was a close call. We have had a few such incidents in our adventures, but I would never try to place the blame on anyone other than myself. No matter who is steering or who is navigating, the responsibility still boils down to one person, the skipper. No one can run a boat aground or put it in jeopardy unless the skipper lets him. However, a very sharp crew member sometimes can make a big contribution toward keeping the skipper out of trouble.

Ferdinand Magellan was the first to come to the Strait, hundreds of others followed, and now here was *Appledore*. Magellan was the first man to organize a sail around the world. Today, the only statue of him is in Punta Arenas.

Ahead of us was a cluster of oil-drilling rigs, some of which were burning off waste gas in huge yellow flames. Tommy was quite impressed. As dawn broke, I talked Tommy into going below for some sleep and told him we would call him when we got close to one. It was then my watch, because I had the 4-to-8, and Doris took the first two hours while I slept.

At 6:00 a.m., Doris woke me and asked, "Which side do you want me to leave the rig ahead of us on?" I said, "Just go between them." Her reply was, "Which ones? You better take a look." I did. What I saw was a continuous line of platforms stretching across the Strait, which was about 10 miles wide at this point. I could make little sense out of them on the chart, so I picked two randomly and we sailed between them. As we were doing this, a man came out on the wing of one, waved, rang a siren, and waved again. I could not quite tell if he was just being friendly or trying to warn me to stand clear, but we had already cleared the two platforms. We made sure to call Tommy.

At this point, it was about 100 miles to Punta Arenas, so I examined the charts for places to anchor come nightfall. Meanwhile, we had picked up a favorable current. Even though it was thickly overcast, the wind had only increased to 20 knots from the west. With a few tacks, we were into the first narrows where the current is reported to be the strongest in the Strait. As luck would have it, we arrived at precisely the right time, as it was beginning to set west. The shoreline showed low tide. With the motor, sails,

Statue of Magellan,
Punta Arenas, Chile.

and current, we flew through the first narrows, making more than 10 knots. Next we started across a 25-mile-wide bay in the rain and fog. At first, we could not even make out the other side, but it cleared some by midmorning, and I could see the point marking the second narrows. Since we still had the current with us, I figured we might be able to reach Punta Arenas by nightfall. I pushed the throttle to full speed ahead.

Off the bow, an unusually large school of dolphins was headed our way. As many as 200 of them surrounded the boat, and they all took turns diving under *Appledore's* bow. Some broke the surface and came clear out of the water. I didn't even have to aim the camera; the viewfinder was full of dolphins.

Late in the afternoon, the wind was increasing from the northwest, a fair breeze for Punta Arenas. We eased the sails and flew. By 6:00 p.m., we had made a good 100 miles in 12 hours. We would be in before

Doris watching dolphins, which often accompanied the schooner.

dark, and it was my turn at the wheel. As I saw Punta Arenas emerge out of the haze, fog, and drizzle, I felt a great surge of excitement. As a teenager, I had read Joshua Slocum's book *Sailing Alone Around the World*, and ever since then, I had wanted to sail to Punta Arenas. My eyes strained through the binoculars to pick up the dock, where we were soon tied up. A friendly Chilean Coast Guardsman came down to clear us in. How fortunate we had been to have such outstanding weather and sea conditions on our passage from Argentina to Chile.

Punta Arenas and High Winds

The following day, February 8, I went to Coast Guard headquarters to apply for a permit to sail in Chilean waters for the next two months. They had no problem honoring this request. Most of the 100,000 Chileans in Punta Arenas have Indian features, since many are descended from the Alacalufes or Yaghan Indian tribes that survived in this harsh environment 400 years earlier with no clothes. It was not until the Europeans came and convinced them to wear clothing that they began dying out, mostly due to pneumonia caused by wearing wet garments. Punta Arenas is a clean town, laid out in blocks, with a statue of Magellan in the main square. The February weather feels like fall in New England, and a strong southwest wind blows almost constantly. Prices in the shops were about the same as in the United States.

In her log, Doris wrote:

> We met Gerry Clark, who had sailed from New Zealand in a 35-foot boat he built and designed. He had already sailed around the Horn and the South Georgia Islands and planned eventually to sail around the world. He laughed when the other members of the crew talked to him about the calm winds we had had. There was a note of skepticism in our voices about the supposed ferocity of the wind in the Strait of Magellan. Gerry had been in force 9 and force 10 conditions several times. For him, the winds had been so severe that the portlights on his cabin sides had gone under water while he was at anchor. We had just taken 12 hours to sail through the same narrows where he had spent four days fighting two gales and sustaining some damage.
>
> We were invited aboard the 200-foot research vessel *Polar Duke*, a new ship crewed by only 12 men that had been built in Norway the previous year and leased to a group of American

(above) Punta Arenas, population 90,000. (below) Sheep ranchers.

Magellanic penguins.

scientists. They were in the process of changing crews, which they did every three months before they headed for the waters off Antarctica. At a picnic we attended on board, the crew filled Lisa's and Tommy's pockets with potato chips and chocolate bars that had been shipped in from the States. The kids were overjoyed.

Juan was a young man of Yugoslavian background whom we met in a restaurant one day. We were having a terrible time trying to get the waitress to understand what we wanted to order. He had been an exchange student in the U.S. for six months, staying with a family in Michigan, so he spoke English very well. He arranged for us to take a taxi to see the penguins at Cape Canelo on the Brunswick Peninsula. On the way, we passed a sheep farm where they were herding several hundred sheep. The men rode beautiful horses, but they depended on their sheepdogs to do much of the herding.

The countryside is barren, except for the pampas grass that feeds the sheep and an occasional ostrich. We stopped to take several pictures. Once the sheep were herded into a corral, one of the men came over and offered to let the kids get on his horse for a picture. Tommy was beside himself with excitement. Lisa was too timid to take him up on his offer. I enjoyed the scene. This lifestyle seemed very romantic. I loved the weather-beaten look of the

Tom and Lisa, with friend, Alexandro.

Chilean's dark face, the thin neat mustache on his upper lip, and the way he let the bottom of his trousers balloon over his shiny leather boots. I felt I had just entered a movie set.

We had to hike about a mile to the coast, where we found at least a hundred penguins guarding the caves they dig in the sand and grass in which to lay their eggs and raise their young. The Magellanic penguin is about 27 inches long and mostly black, except for a broad, white band on each side of the head and the chest. The minute we got near, most of them scurried to the nearest cave and hid. Four of them refused to hide and ran about frantically till they were too exhausted to move. The chicks were as large as their parents. Their first layers of feathers had fallen off in their latest molt. The ground was so completely covered with the feathers that it looked as though it had snowed. One cute fellow, half in and half out of a cave, mocked me by shaking his head left and right as I did. After laying their eggs in September and October, the birds stay until March, when they leave to go up to the southern Brazilian coast for the winter.

Tommy and Lisa made a friend of their own, Alexandro, 14, the nephew of the owner of the fishing boat we were tied up to. Every day he would come to play with Tommy. Regardless of the fact that he could speak no English nor we Spanish, they seemed to have a good time. Alexandro carved a small boat that he named Michael, and Tommy, not to be outdone, made a boat from a crate he found. For several days, they played side by side, sailing their boats.

The gales we experienced while tied up to the dock instilled a healthy respect in all of us. It was still a long way to the Pacific. We realized the intensity of the wind even while trying to walk along the street. We had to clutch Lisa for fear she would be blown away.

Two days before departing Punta Arenas, the wind shifted to the northeast, and we were blown onto the 80-year-old fishing boat that we had rafted up to. The usual southerly wind had been holding us off quite nicely, but now we rolled and pounded the boat. To add to the problem, the fisherman tried to help us by slacking off our stern line. When he did this, our bow swung in, and our railcap cracked on one especially big roll.

To make matters worse, I could not get underway because I had taken apart the fuel filter, which had a cracked bowl. The replacement would not arrive until the next day. Everyone was up on deck to help fend off while I dug the pieces of the old fuel filter out of the trash and made a fast jury repair. We then got underway, which solved our problems. Later in the morning, while we were tied up to the other side of the pier, a pilot told us we had only two hours to move back before the wind would start to blow hard from the south. I took his advice, and it was fortunate I did. He was correct in his forecast, and it was blowing a gale by evening.

We had a pleasant 10-day stay in Punta Arenas, where we were able to receive mail through the British consulate. Our crew stayed ashore most of the time in a room at the Magellan Hotel that cost $4 a day. We asked if anyone would like to be replaced, since others wanted to join us, but everyone wanted to continue. Their courage and determination impressed me. Doris and I were totally committed, but it would have been easy for them to give it up.

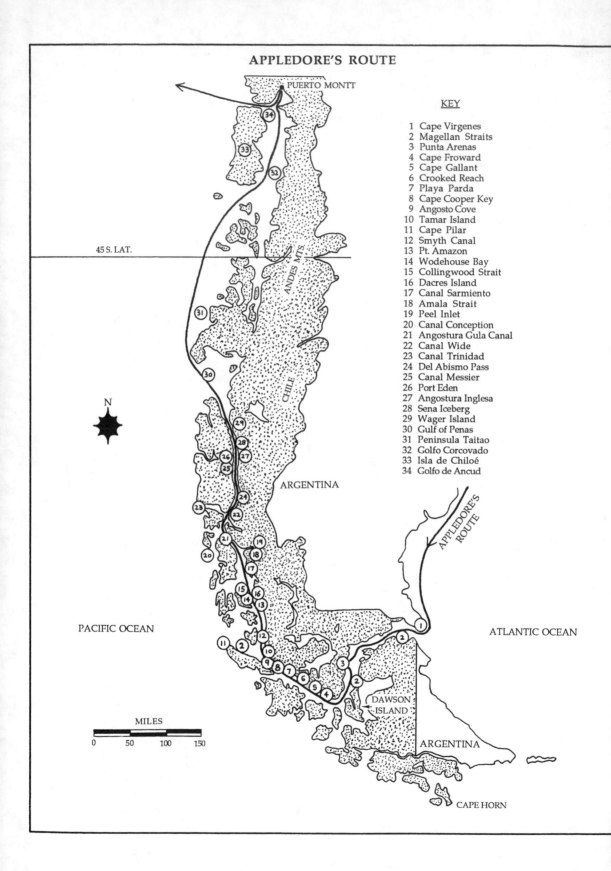

APPLEDORE'S ROUTE

PUERTO MONTT

KEY

1 Cape Virgenes
2 Magellan Straits
3 Punta Arenas
4 Cape Froward
5 Cape Gallant
6 Crooked Reach
7 Playa Parda
8 Cape Cooper Key
9 Angosto Cove
10 Tamar Island
11 Cape Pilar
12 Smyth Canal
13 Pt. Amazon
14 Wodehouse Bay
15 Collingwood Strait
16 Dacres Island
17 Canal Sarmiento
18 Amala Strait
19 Peel Inlet
20 Canal Conception
21 Angostura Gula Canal
22 Canal Wide
23 Canal Trinidad
24 Del Abismo Pass
25 Canal Messier
26 Port Eden
27 Angostura Inglesa
28 Sena Iceberg
29 Wager Island
30 Gulf of Penas
31 Peninsula Taitao
32 Golfo Corcovado
33 Isla de Chiloé
34 Golfo de Ancud

45 S. LAT.

ANDES MTS.

CHILE

N

ARGENTINA

APPLEDORE'S ROUTE

PACIFIC OCEAN

ATLANTIC OCEAN

DAWSON ISLAND

ARGENTINA

MILES

0   50   100   150

CAPE HORN

The Strait of Magellan

At 4:00 a.m. on February 17, the wind stopped blowing and the motion of the boat woke me. A slight swell was coming in from the north, causing us to roll just as we had done when we cracked the railcap. Since I had cleared with the Chilean Coast Guard the night before, we got underway. I spent the first half hour spinning our compass, which was off 8°.

The morning was calm as we motored south toward Cape Froward, the southernmost tip of South America, at 53° 54' south lattitude. By midmorning, the wind picked up from the southeast, bringing in some fog, but most of it had burned off by noon. At 3:00 p.m., we were passing Cape Froward, a bold, black headland that slopes sharply down from a 3,018-foot summit. There was a dusting of snow on the top, although not nearly as much as on the mountains on Dawson Island, to our south. Several waterfalls cascaded along the cliffs, and all hands were on deck to witness the spectacle.

At 4:00 p.m., we were 20 miles from a safe anchorage, but the current was turning against us and the fog was starting to close in. Two hours later, we picked up Cape Gallant Light, knowing our chosen anchorage was only a short distance from there, but by the time we reached the light, darkness had descended. We looked in vain for a small island off the spit of land where the pass was located but could not distinguish the island from the point. Low, black clouds blocked even the faintest illumination that the stars would provide on a clear night. We even had to feel our way around the deck. When Ray Corbett, who was sounding with the leadline, called back 11 feet, I put the engine in reverse. Just then, a gust of wind hit us, threatening to drive us ashore, but full reverse was enough and we backed off. We had to settle for anchoring in 55 feet of water outside the point.

At 4:00 the next morning, it was light enough to get underway. With the wind dead against us at 25 knots, we started tacking, using only

Approaching Crooked Reach.

Doris at the helm.

Day, Bob and Chris.

reefed mainsail and staysail. At this point, the Strait was only a couple of miles wide, and progress was slow because we had to tack so often. At 6:00 a.m., the sun began breaking through the thick layer of clouds, and patches of sunlight appeared on the high, jagged mountain peaks that lined both sides of the Strait.

We were approaching Crooked Reach, a narrow passage that marks the meeting point of Atlantic and Pacific waters. At this point the Strait makes an S-turn, and when I was halfway through it, I saw a white cloudbank coming toward us. In my naiveté, I put on my raingear, expecting merely to get wet. Then the wind came, a blast of frigid Antarctic air. I yelled down to Doris for help, then ran forward to release the main peak halyard. Doris was up within seconds, and by then the wind was howling at 50 knots. The main dropped into the lazyjacks and we ran forward to drop the staysail. With the cold wind increasing, *Appledore* was out of control and racing toward shore.

There was so much white spindrift in the air that it was impossible to see in any direction. I had to run back to the wheel as Doris and Kate, who joined her now, tackled the staysail. It was too late to save the staysail from shaking off its lashings. It was perpendicular to the bow and flogging violently. In fact, the whole boat was shaking. Fortunately, the boom was still on board. If I had jibed to get away from the rapidly approaching shore, which I could not see yet, Doris and Kate both would have been thrown overboard. I yelled, "Hurry!" even though I knew they were doing the best they could. I engaged the engine full speed ahead trying to keep the bow up into the wind, but that did nothing. Finally, the sail was down and under control, and I threw the wheel over. We jibed with such a heeling force that dishes crashed in the galley, but at least I could now steer out into the middle of the channel, where the initial blast of wind had died to a more comfortable 45 knots. We quickly set the reefed foresail and started beating west. Once you gain an inch in the Strait of Magellan, it's hard to give it up.

During the afternoon, we made little progress, and when another white squall came rolling down the Strait, we were able to tack into a small bay behind Cape Rosario. We sounded with our leadline and found it deep, so decided to cross the Strait to Butler Bay. But after an hour of no progress against wind and current, we returned to Rosario Bay and, in 70 feet of water, dropped our 75-pound plow anchor with 200 pounds of 5/8-inch chain and 300 feet of one-inch nylon line. It held, and we put the skiff over the side to clean the hull, which had black smudges from the tire fenders used in Punta Arenas.

The next morning was rainy and the wind was only 20 knots, so we got underway with the three reefed lower sails set. At best, we were making three miles to the west on two tacks, which took about 90 minutes. Every hour, a squall would come through, increasing the wind to 40 knots. This wind was the coldest we had yet felt, and hail frequently came with it, tearing at our faces. I was wearing two shirts, two sweaters, a winter jacket, and complete foul-weather raingear, yet I was still cold.

By midafternoon, we had made 18 miles, and Playa Parda, our chosen anchorage, was still 10 miles away. After our experience at Port Gallant two nights earlier, and with squalls coming at us more frequently with higher and higher gusts, it was with relief that just before dusk we approached the narrow entrance to Playa Parda Bay. Once inside, we were surrounded by towering 3,000-foot cliffs, with waterfalls rushing down from the even higher glacial icecap behind them. Although we could not see the icecap from inside the bay, we had seen it when entering, and the chill in the air continued to remind us that it was there.

The cliffs were clad in green vegetation climbing halfway up, and it was barren rock from there on. Being so small in comparison to our surroundings, we felt a sense of loneliness. In this perfectly enclosed basin, about 500 yards in diameter, we expected to find ample shelter, but the wind funneling off the cliffs taught us what real williwaws were. These cold blasts of wind last only seconds, but they reach hurricane force. If we were on deck, we often had to hold on tight, and sometimes they came from two different directions at once.

Kate and Chris, Playa Parda.

The following day, it was raining hard, so we all slept in while our diesel-fired Dickerson galley stove made everything comfortable and dry below. No one complained about the heat. Now and then, we would hear a williwaw cry in the rigging and the schooner suddenly would heel over. When the sun came out briefly in the afternoon, we went ashore.

The land was incredibly lush, with strange wildflowers, mosses, and gnarled trees. Where there was life here, there seemed to be too much life. A beautiful kingfisher sat on a branch ruffling his feathers and watched us with inquisitive eyes. A thick layer of bog covered the ground, making walking difficult. It felt like walking on a sponge, or perhaps a bowl of Jell-O. I was concerned that Tommy and Lisa might fall through and disappear, so we did not venture far inland. Instead, we climbed a rocky hill overlooking the harbor for a spectacular view. Below us was *Appledore,* a white pearl reflected in a green sea. Behind was the Strait of Magellan, torn up by the wind. Farther to the south were the snow-capped peaks of Tierra del Fuego.

The next day at 4:00 a.m., we departed Playa Parda and began beating west toward the Pacific. After the crew helped hoist the anchor and sails, they went back to their warm bunks. In two hours, we had made five miles, and a choppy sea began making up. It was the kind of chop that usually precedes wind, but again not knowing what to expect, I carried on. At this point the coast, as desolate as any I have ever seen, had a stark beauty. Black clouds surrounded the peaks and spread down low. I couldn't decide whether to seek shelter at once or to push on. I decided to turn around and head back to Playa Parda, but when I did, the wind felt weak on my back, so I swung the schooner back up into the wind and continued to beat, although we were making little progress.

Just as Doris was coming up to relieve me, I was in the process of again making the same indecisive maneuver. "What are you doing?" she asked. After I told her, she said simply, "Well, make up your mind." By then, I did not have to make a decision. The storm came as a black squall, with 40 knots of wind that increased rapidly. We got the sails down and ran before it under bare poles. The spindrift was awesome. In minutes, we were approaching the entrance to Playa Parda, but first we would have to clear Shelter Island, a maneuver that would put us slightly downwind of the entrance. We would never make it, I figured, without the sails to drive us. Therefore, as we passed Shelter Island, I came up into the wind with full speed ahead on the engine. We quickly set the reefed foresail, then fell off. *Appledore* responded and came out from behind the lee of the island with a bone in her teeth. I couldn't have gotten any more speed out of her if I had installed a 5,000-h.p. engine. We shot across the Strait toward the entrance, which was fringed with rocks. I knew we would have only one chance; either we would pass safely into the harbor or we would come to an abrupt halt outside. Sliding to leeward, we began to make the final approach, and I cut the engine to slow our speed. This was a mistake, since it made us slide to leeward even more. I quickly pushed the throttle to full ahead. Without exaggerating, I would say the wind was 45 to 50 knots. We surged past rocks on both sides, just below the surface, as we once again entered this refuge. Inside, tremendous blasts of wind hit us from all directions, bouncing off the high cliffs, but at least we were protected from swells. We dropped anchor and waltzed around as gusts of wind in excess of 60 knots blasted us.

From Doris's log:

> In the morning, it looked as if we had dragged anchor a couple of hundred feet. We reset the anchor, but when Herb backed full astern with the engine, it did not hold. The women manned the windlass again. I do not quite remember how the tradition got started, but the women on board pumped the handles and basically got the anchor up every time we got underway. Chris was in charge of preparing the anchor and chain for being dropped and pulling the anchor on board once the girls had it up to the waterline, and he did a good job. The rest of the men laid back as the girls got in their exercise. Everyone seemed happy with the arrangement.

Chris preparing the anchor.

A few minutes later, we dropped anchor again. I could see everyone cringe as Herb slammed the engine in reverse. I thought I could hear people muttering, "Why does he do that? He'll pull it out again!" But he was determined to set it well so he could get a good night's sleep. We kept a night anchor watch but were never quite sure at this early stage in the voyage whether some crew members knew how to determine if we were dragging.

Tommy was the only one happy to be at anchor. He was getting good at card games, especially poker. It was not quite the education I wanted him to have, but I guess I could rationalize and say it helped him in his math.

This time we spent four days in Playa Parda and became keen cloud watchers, staring at the sky as clouds skittered across at alarming speeds. Often in the morning Herb would think that they had backed to the southwest and we would be able to leave, but by midday, they would again be tearing out of the northwest, the worst possible direction.

Conditions on board were deteriorating. Everyone was getting punchy. The slightest thing would set off an argument. I heard a couple of people arguing over who had not been flushing the toilet properly. Our toilet was hand pumped, and if you did not pump it at least 15 strokes, the water would not clear. One person even complained that someone had been making too much noise with his spoon as he ate his breakfast cereal.

The women decided things would be better if we all took baths in a stream, so, like Amazons, we plunged into the 38° water. It was an invigorating experience.

Daytime temperatures were not all that cold, averaging about 54°. Ice never formed on the deck, although several squalls came through with sleet and hail. Even at night, it never went below freezing. It was the windchill factor that kept us cold when on deck. Our record-low barometer reading was 28.9 inches.

On February 24, with the wind northwest at 25 knots, we got underway. Squalls were coming about every hour, but we were able to carry the three lower sails and made some progress on the swift outgoing current. By midafternoon, the current turned against us, so we tacked into Port Angosto, approached by a narrow channel. It is worth the effort, because there are majestic waterfalls on both sides. The harbor was not without williwaws, though, and again we had to have a night anchor watch. From this point on, we kept an anchor watch at night until we were north of Port Eden.

Port Angosto seemed to be a popular anchorage. Handpainted signs from other boats hung on trees, but we did not see one from the famous vessel *Spray*, skippered by Joshua Slocum, which stopped in 1896. By 6:00 p.m., the anchorage was peaceful, rather remarkable for the Strait of Magellan. The williwaws were gone and the wind came in light gusts. Doris had made chicken soup with the last fresh chicken we had bought in Punta Arenas, and we had cherry pie for dessert. As darkness came, water thundered down the vertical rock formations, drowning out all of the other natural sounds. The chart showed a small cut into another small bay, but our desire to move on was greater than our desire to explore.

Most of the crew members were suffering from colds or mild bouts of dysentery. This weather was rough on the body. In their book *The Last Sailors*, Neil Hollander and Harald Mertes quoted a captain who plied the waters of the Patagonia Channels carrying wood to Puerto Montt. The man said, "It is impossible to get warm. Always it is wet and raw. A little sun warms you one minute. The next you have a hailstone poking you in the eyes as you try to see what's ahead of you."

Doris had just finished reading *Mutiny on the Bounty*. "I don't know what we are all complaining about," she said. "We are in heaven compared to those men. At least we all have our teeth and you haven't resorted to carrying around a cat-o'-nine-tails or having us flogged."

Sail training ship Esmeralda, *Patagonia Channels.*

On Monday, February 25, Ray woke me for my watch and I glanced out the hatch. In the dim light, I could see the clouds moving from south to north. Finally the wind was coming from a direction that would do us some good, since the Strait runs northwest from this point. Now we would stand a chance of making it out of the Strait and north into the Smyth Canal.

As I wakened the crew, a flash of lightning illuminated the main companionway, but there was no thunder, so I thought it must be a long way off, perhaps down by Cape Horn. Once we got back out into the Strait, the wind was southwest at only 10 knots — practically dead calm for these waters. I used the engine to make as much westward progress as possible before the current turned against us. I could not help but think of others who had traveled this route without auxiliary diesel power, although a fair breeze would come eventually. The worst record for a passage by sail through the Strait is 86 days. In 1581, Magellan's fleet left Spain with 25 ships. Thirty months later, only five ships were left when they reached the entrance to the Strait of Magellan. Some gave up trying to reach the Pacific and returned to Spain. Some settled in the area, but only a handful of men were alive when others arrived six years later. The only three ships that had made it through were with Magellan, and they were in poor condition.

Our calm was short-lived. Soon the wind was blowing again from the northwest at 30 knots, carrying rain with it. This continued throughout the day, but we were making progress with a favorable current. As we sailed past our first alternate anchorage behind Cape Providence, the wind came up strong. It was discouraging. Ahead, between the squalls, I could see Cape Tamar, around which we had to sail before turning north to enter the Smyth Canal. Things improved at midday, although the seas were building from the west. One more tack and we would clear Tamar Island, be able to sail off the wind, and steer north for the Smyth Canal. The seas were breaking and boiling on the reefs surrounding Tamar Island, and another rain squall was coming our way. We made the tack and eased the sheets, picking up speed. For the first time since departing Punta Arenas, we had a fair breeze. But the squall overtook us, and although we were running downwind with everything reefed, we still had too much sail up. As we flew past Fairway Island and into Smyth Canal, the two lighthouse keepers stationed on Fairway waved at us.

We took advantage of the fair wind, although it was not easy. Squalls overtook us every hour, and some came with hail, which bounced off the deck like artillery fire. It even began to accumulate. Just as darkness was closing in, we dropped anchor at Bahia Fortuna and went below to warm up. I had not expected to have such a good day; we were a long way up the canal.

Patagonia Channels and Puerto Montt

I wondered where Chilean naval headquarters had us pinned on their chart. Before we left Punta Arenas, we had had to submit a route and time plan to obtain a permit to sail through the Strait. They kept track of each boat's whereabouts with colored pins on a detailed wall chart.

The next morning, we left again at dawn and reached our next anchorage at Wodehouse Bay. There was little swinging room, however, and the water was deep, so we continued on to Occasion Bay.

That night turned into a nightmare for the watches. Heavy rain and winds of 40 knots rocked the boat. The sky was so black that I doubted anyone knew what they were seeing. You would flash the light on the shore and, as Doris remarked, "It actually scared you!" It seemed as though we could reach out and touch the steep cliffs. I hoped we would not drag in earnest, because we probably would have hit the shore before anyone was the wiser. To make matters worse, the holding ground was poor. We had to reset the anchor three times before it held well. I am reluctant to set two anchors when the wind keeps shifting like it was here. During the night we circled around the anchor perhaps five times. Because of the high cliffs the wind was constantly changing direction.

The following morning, we got underway. Ahead of us were hundreds of miles of natural canals, bays, and glaciers that were reputed to have some fantastic scenery. Each mile northward seemed to give us an improvement in the weather. But we still had a strong northwest wind for the first two days, requiring some hard tacking, so progress was slow. We anchored each night, realizing it would be difficult to navigate the Patagonia Channels in the dark. The nights were black when it was cloudy, which was 90 percent of the time, and the rain we experienced was something else: 5 or 6 inches in as many hours.

In the Sarmiento Canal, strong winds came against us. The canals act as a funnel, so the wind is either behind you or against you. We found

Appledore *among icebergs, Peel Inlet.*

an anchorage at Dacres Island, a spot that reminded me of Maine. The islands here were far lower than the 5,000-foot mountains we had been anchoring behind, so we had good shelter with no williwaws. We felt the true wind on our bow and pointed up into it for two days, waiting for it to change direction. To occupy our time we made desserts along with 5 pounds of fudge.

Finally the wind changed to the southwest and we got underway early, sailing without the engine. Along with the 25-knot wind, we had some hail, sleet, and rain. But as long as the wind was at our backs, we didn't care. We literally flew up the channel. Around midmorning, the sun came out for a while, which felt good on our faces. On several occasions, we lost the wind or had it briefly come against us as we made a sharp turn behind a headland, yet this was by far our best day's sail since leaving Punta Arenas.

By late afternoon, we reached Peel Inlet, where we were able to ease the sheets and sail, heading due west. After making a turn into Amala Sound, we spotted our first glacier. This was a 20-mile detour from the main channel, but it was well worth it. By then, darkness had fallen, and we found an anchorage with good holding across from the glacier in Caleta Amelia Cove. Several steamer ducks skittered across the water alongside us, easily keeping up with our 4 knots as we sailed to the anchorage. I had read several accounts describing people eating these oily, foul-tasting birds, but we were happy to stick to our canned chicken.

Amelia Cove was the most tranquil spot we had found since leaving Punta Arenas two weeks earlier. There was no wind and much more vegetation. The water was a milky color, caused by sediment from the glacier, and there was no ice. We had heard about other boats not being able to get within three miles of this cove because of pack ice. During the night, several cracks that sounded like gunshots were heard, caused by the moving glacier and the icebergs calving off.

Early the next morning, it was easy to forget we were a mere 150 miles from the Strait of Magellan. Birds were singing, brooks were trickling in the woods, and the emerald reflections of trees made for a tranquil setting. Across the bay, however, was the huge blue glacier emptying large pieces of ice into the water. Beyond it were tall, jagged mountains covered with snow, their peaks piercing the clouds. With the skiff, Tommy and I used this early-morning quiet as an opportunity to photograph the steamer ducks. For some odd reason, they cannot fly, and when aroused, they beat their wings like paddle wheels, propelling themselves across the water. If you have chased them long enough, they escape by diving below the surface and staying down for several minutes. We got some good motion-picture footage and then went over to the glacier for a closer inspection with *Appledore* following behind us. The blue tint in the rough, jagged ice is unusually colorful. While we were there, hundreds of tons of ice calved off, sending a groundswell out to the boat. Tommy and I were separated from *Appledore* only by a couple of hundred yards, yet we had to work our way carefully through the ice and fend off many bergs to get back. We could not get closer than a half-mile to the glacier, but that was close enough.

At one point, *Appledore* was surrounded by "bergy" bits, and I went out on a large berg to take a picture. Because our propeller is fully exposed to any ice coming in under the counter, we did not back up but went ahead slowly and moved the ice out of the way, as an icebreaker would do. We parked the bow of *Appledore* on one iceberg and held it there with the engine on slow ahead while the crew took turns getting off and taking pictures. The slight throttle actually started turning the iceberg around. By the end of the day, after seeing all we had come for, we resumed our voyage northward.

For the next few days, it rained steadily, forcing Tommy and Lisa to stay below decks. Like any children 8 and 4 years old, they had a great deal of energy to burn off, but the rest of the crew wanted it quiet so they could sleep most of the day. I had forgotten how much sleep young people seem to need. I think they were storing up their energy for our

Appledore crew getting out on iceberg.

arrival in port, because once in port, an incredible metamorphosis would take place: instead of needing 12 to 14 hours of sleep a day, they could do fine with four or five (although I realize the sleep on board was escape from boredom).

Since we had used our engine a great deal, we needed more fuel, which we found at Port Eden, population 388. How fortunate we were to obtain it there, no matter what the price, for our next stop was 500 miles away at Puerto Montt. It never cleared up while at Port Eden, and I wondered who would want to live there, yet the small settlement has been there for centuries.

A derelict Chilean navy ship served as headquarters for the local customs and police officials. Boats go alongside to check in. About a hundred houses, arranged in a horseshoe shape along the shore, are painted blue or green with blue trim — a colorful contrast to the drab terrain. There were no roads, just a muddy path meandering past the houses.

When we went ashore to trade with the local people, I noticed that they all burned wood for heat. Most of the homes had no storm windows, but the cold didn't seem to bother the locals as it does Europeans. In Port Eden I had an example of how great the Chilean people are. In my pocket was a new wool hat that I used while sailing,

Port Eden, population 388.

and it dropped out during my walk around the village. When I noticed it was missing, I retraced my steps and asked along the way if anyone had found it. Back near the dock, a woman pointed to a tree beside the path and there it was, hanging on a conspicuous branch waiting to be retrieved by its owner. It was a nice feeling visiting these secluded, honest people who had never even seen a television set. Their diet consists mostly of fish and mussels, the shells of which are used on all the paths to keep them from becoming too muddy.

Since we were three weeks behind schedule, we only stayed a day at Port Eden. On a voyage such as this, it is crucial to be in the right season. Once you linger too long, you are forced to wait out the hurricane seasons and resume the voyage a year later.

Our next passage, from Port Eden to Puerto Montt, was to be outside most of the way, with one stop at another glacier, Seno Iceberg. We went outside the channels at the Gulf of Pain and encountered winds in excess of 40 knots. Here we experienced the huge swells from the great Southern Ocean. Sailing with only our reefed foresail, we made little progress for 12 hours. The seas were mountainous, 30 or more feet from crest to trough. After a day of rough going, the wind backed to the southwest and we were off sailing northward along the west coast of Chile, making great time.

On the evening of Tuesday, March 12, we approached the southern end of Corcovado Sound from the sea. Our Sat-Nav was having some trouble, but we set a course from our last good position that would bring us into the middle of the sound. Darkness was falling and time was running out for making a safe anchorage. I had picked out one spot behind Grand Guaiteca Island, but as we approached, I could not determine where it was. The sea was breaking so ferociously on the surrounding rocks that the surface was covered with white foam for a good distance out. The muffled thunder of the crashing waves called out to me, keep clear, this was no place for a little wooden schooner to anchor for the evening. Instead, we set a course for the middle of the sound, where we would stay until morning, making our way northward at dead slow ahead. I could not help but think of the Norwegian solo sailor Al Hansen. He vanished in this area without a trace in his thirty-six foot wooden double ender *Mary Jane* after being the first singlehander to round Cape Horn in 1934. I would like to think his spirit was sailing with us in these waters. Remarkably he had no auxiliary power.

Once into the sound, the waters became calm — a relief from the thrashing we had been taking for the previous three days. But now we had a new problem to contend with — thick fog. As darkness and fog descended, our running lights reflected off the heavy mist to illuminate the decks.

Fortunately, the Sat-Nav threw out our position every so often. As I marked the positions on the chart, we proceeded right up the middle of the sound. Without this instrument, matters would have been much different. A fail-safe mechanism on the instrument tells you if it is not working or if the position it calculates is in error, so I felt pretty good about relying on its accuracy. The evening was quiet and calm, and with the engine on slow ahead, we would also be able to hear any breaking surf or other vessels in the area. Around 2:00 a.m., some kelp got caught in the propeller, but we quickly shook it off by reversing and going forward a few times.

At dawn, Corcovado Sound was like a sheet of glass, and we could just make out the dim outline of Chiloé Island to port. When Doris relieved me, I gave her instructions to steer 320° for a fairway buoy approximately 10 miles ahead. When she got to it, I told her to change course 60° to 020°. I had not had much sleep, so I went below and slept without setting the alarm clock. When I woke up in a couple of hours, Doris was below, having been relieved by the next watch. The sun was shining through the hatchway and the atmosphere felt good on board. When I asked her what time she had changed course at the fairway buoy, she said they had not seen it yet. A quick calculation in my head told me we should have passed it already. I jumped up on deck and looked around. The fairway buoy was nowhere to be seen, and, not having

Appledore *in Gulf of Ancud.*

changed course yet, we were getting close to a 3-foot shoal. Full reverse stopped us dead in our tracks, and I peered over the side. I couldn't see the bottom, so we made the course change and proceeded slowly ahead. Sometimes you just get lucky.

That morning, I felt an uplifting of morale on *Appledore*. We were about to sail into Puerto Montt and leave behind the cold Strait of Magellan and the Patagonia Channels.

Puerto Montt, Chile, is about 35 miles inland from the Pacific, at the northern end of the Gulf of Ancud. As we sailed toward it, we could see large fields with sheep and cattle grazing, quaint barns and buildings scattered over the hillsides, and people on horseback. Each small island or peninsula had a neatly kept homestead with smoke spiraling from a chimney. It was a beautiful sight after the desolate terrain of the Strait. There was something comforting about seeing human organization in the patchwork landscape.

In one small cove just before Puerto Montt, we dropped anchor as we ran out of daylight. The late sun raked in under some dark clouds, casting yellow patterns over the hills. A man leaning casually against a fencepost watched us as we furled the sails, and soon two men in a wooden rowboat came out to meet us. They were very friendly, as we found all Chileans to be, but they could not speak English, which, unfortunately is

Farmers coming in from outer islands, Puerto Montt.

the only language I know. Tommy, Lisa, and I went ashore with them to try to find someone to speak with. No one else wanted to go.

Once ashore, we met the man who was still leaning against the fence, both arms outstretched along the rail and completely relaxed and open to strangers. I waved, and without a moment's hesitation, he returned my gesture. I felt good about these Chilean homesteaders and wished we had more time to spend with them. It was impossible to speak to anyone ashore because of the language barrier, but our minds communicated. We saw two small boys riding together on horseback and some nice-looking Holstein cows pastured with a bull. As it grew late, we had to return to the boat, but it felt good to have mud on our feet. The same two men who brought us ashore rowed us back to *Appledore* as the sun set across the sound.

Late the next afternoon, we approached Puerto Montt, our first big city in many weeks. As Lisa came up the hatch, I said, "Look over there, Lisa." When she turned and looked, her eyes were filled with astonishment and excitement. "Look at all those lights and cars," I said, and for a moment she was speechless. For many weeks she had seen only mountains, seals, penguins, glaciers, and waterfalls. It certainly had been an experience we would never forget.

Puerto Montt, with a population of about 100,000, was not on our original itinerary. We stopped there for supplies and diesel fuel because

Lancha, *Puerto Montt fishing and cargo sloop.*

Tahiti was 5,000 miles away, with no sure prospect of obtaining stores at our next scheduled ports of call. We had also heard that it would be an interesting place to visit.

We tied up to a short navy pier, and, due to a 15- to 20-foot tide, it was a good 20 feet up a steel ladder to the top. We left plenty of slack in our lines, but at midnight we found it was not enough. We began to heel to starboard as the inboard lines took a strain and began to lift the boat out of the water. Fortunately, we had tied the lines properly and could slack them off quickly. With the tide out, it was surprising to see the banks dry out and the harbor change from a good-sized bay to a small river.

Puerto Montt still has a traditional wooden windjammer fleet, and in the morning, the harbor was bustling as these vessels loaded and unloaded. Most of the 40-foot cutters, called *lanchas*, have no engine, and they carry firewood, planks, potatoes, and livestock from the remote islands and villages to Puerto Montt. Once the boats are grounded out, horse-drawn wagons go down on the flats beside them and offload the cargo to deliver it to the merchants. Along the waterfront, they are still building these traditional *lanchas*. In one shop, four were under construction. The boatbuilders showed great interest in *Appledore*, which was anchored in front of their shops. They checked her out quite thoroughly and one builder said *Appledore* had the perfect sheer. Hearing such flattering comments, I gave him a complete set of plans, knowing that would meet with Bud McIntosh's approval. Perhaps Bud's influence will now be felt in Chile.

We were only able to tie up downtown for a couple of days, after which we were asked to move to the yacht club, several miles downriver. Although it was a small, inactive club, the members treated us well. We were finally able to do our laundry, washing it in buckets under a spigot.

During our 10-day stay, we took a bus ride 80 miles north and were amazed at all the open fields with grazing cattle. Almost all were black-and-white Holsteins, but we did see a few Guernsey herds. We had thought of Chile as mountainous, yet there is plenty of flat land many miles inland from the Pacific coast. In the distance, we saw the great snow-capped Andes, and, much closer, 8,790-foot Mt. Osorno, with a very recognizable volcanic cone that is similar to Japan's Mount Fuji, except that it is covered with snow 100 percent of the time.

Since leaving Maine, we had exposed more than 20,000 feet of motion-picture film, wanting to be sure of good coverage of the Strait of Magellan. It had been hard work, and the producer had yet to come up with any of the money he had promised. Doris and I had spent a few hundred dollars of our own to get the footage, and every time we air-freighted the film out, it was a major problem to get it to an airport and through customs. In Puerto Montt, Doris was upset with me for mailing out all of the footage, even after I explained that it would go bad if we kept it on board. She still had not forgiven me for not getting an advance, and she was doing much of the work in carrying around the camera equipment. I told her that the money would be coming. While in Puerto Montt, I made several calls to the producer, who assured me that it would be in my account by the end of the week.

Tommy finally found a solution to the boredom and the necessity for being quiet at sea — books. Almost overnight, he had developed an insatiable appetite for reading. At this point, we had only a dozen children's books on board, so once he had read and reread them several times, we picked through stories in the condensed *Reader's Digest*. By the time we arrived back in Boothbay Harbor, his library would include more than 200 titles. At least 60 of them were by an English author by the name of Enid Blyton. The children in her books became his playmates.

His favorite book, however, was one given to us by Dave and Marion Dash, former members of the first world voyage. It was *Clear the Bridge,* by Admiral Richard O'Kane. Her brother had served with O'Kane on board the submarine *Tang* and was lost when the vessel was torpedoed. Tommy read the book several times.

Lisa was still in the observer stage. She loved to watch people and have them around, but she did not seem to feel the need to have playmates. Also, being a cute little girl did not hurt her popularity on board. When our crew left *Appledore* to enjoy the ports, she often looked bored and dejected.

Trading with the locals, Marquesas, Appledore II.

Into the South Pacific

We left Puerto Montt for the South Pacific on March 23, after restocking *Appledore* with 300 pounds of fresh Chilean potatoes, 50 pounds of oranges, 50 pounds of vegetables, 25 pounds of frozen hamburger, and 10 frozen chickens. Our little 12-volt DC Norcold refrigerator kept the meat cold for two weeks, just long enough for us to eat everything before it spoiled. It was such a luxury to have the fresh meat. On our first world trip, we had used mainly canned meats, but on that trip, the dollar had been very weak, and there were few ports where we did not lose out on the exchange rate.

Back in the Pacific, we immediately encountered a northeast gale that lasted a day, after which we got a fair southerly wind. At dawn on the fifth day, just six hours before landfall on Robinson Crusoe Island, our satellite navigator stopped working. It would not lock on to a satellite. It had worked almost perfectly since leaving Maine, except in the Strait of Magellan, where we could not rely on its accuracy because the channels were too narrow and the charts were often inaccurate. It had become another crew member and friend, and it was letting me down at a crucial moment.

When it was light enough to see, Robinson Crusoe Island was on the horizon, and we just needed to sail up to it and around to the northeast side, where we dropped anchor in Cumberland Bay. Only 12 miles long and four miles wide, the island has sheer cliffs as its predominant feature. On this island, able-bodied seaman Alexander Selkirk was marooned from 1704 to 1709. He complained to the captain of his ship that it was not fit for sea and he wanted to be put ashore. The captain obliged. When the crew cast him ashore, he changed his mind, but he could not convince the captain to reconsider. Selkirk survived on wild goats, berries, and fish. He wore out his knife and made another one from a piece of iron that he ground down to an edge. Later, Daniel Defoe used Selkirk's accounts for his book *Robinson Crusoe*.

135

Drying the laundry, off Juan Fernandez (Robinson Crusoe) Island.

Today there are about 500 people making their living, mostly from lobstering, on Robinson Crusoe Island. They sell the lobsters on the mainland at a very good profit. It cost us $13 (U.S.) for four spiny lobsters. They use small, wooden, double-ended boats with a motor well for a long-shaft Swedish outboard. There is no harbor here, and when the wind comes up from the north, they have to haul the boats out quickly by skidding them ashore. And it can get rough fast. We only stayed two days, and the wind got up to 45 knots during the night, creating a large swell with which we rolled dramatically. I used our trusted 75-pound CQR plow anchor with 55 feet of 5/8-inch chain and 300 feet of one-inch nylon line. It held well and was the only anchor that we had set since leaving Maine. I had two 75-pound plows and two 100-pound Paul Luke fisherman anchors on board.

Semitropical Robinson Crusoe is also called the island of flowers, and it lived up to its name. Its banks are covered with wild geraniums, lilies, trumpet vines, and blackberries, exuding a fragrance that one can truly appreciate after having been out to sea.

On our passage from Robinson Crusoe to Easter Island, about 1,800 miles, we went almost directly north until reaching latitude 27° south. Then we sailed west to Easter Island. It was one of the greatest passages that we have ever made. Not once did the wind come from forward of the beam, and the seas were practically flat, with a 10-to-15-knot breeze almost all the way, except for a three-day stretch that was dead calm. For navigation, we used our old friends Antares, Canopus, Acrux, Regulus, Sirius, and Betelgeuse. The satellite navigator had packed up for good. Perhaps this was a blessing, because close observation of the complexity of our universe cannot help but be inspiring.

Easter Island has no harbor, so we anchored on the lee side, but the swell found its way into the anchorage, and we rolled more than if we had been at sea with sails set. It was a thrill to go ashore with our little skiff and 4-h.p. Seagull outboard motor. We put the kids in life jackets. After the first night when we nearly swamped the skiff, we decided it was best not to go in after dark.

This unique island is owned and governed by Chile. Most of the people speak only Spanish, but I met an islander who had spent several months at UCLA and had married an American. We found him extremely helpful in arranging to get fuel and water. The second day we were there, his father took us in his Volkswagen bus to see the island's famous statues and caves. First we saw the caves where the "Long Ears" had lived. These primitive people were distinguished by long earlobes formed by stretching the lobes with bone inserts, and they ruled the island at the time the statues were carved. At one time, there were as many as 20,000 people living on Easter Island. The caves, made of flat stones stacked one atop the other, had openings that were so tiny we had to climb on our hands and knees to get into them. Once inside, however, there was plenty of standing headroom. Rocks and boulders overlooking the cliffs were full of hieroglyphics.

The first statues we saw were lying face down on the side of the road. Lisa commented, "They look like they are crying." These statues had been left there when civil war broke out between the long-eared rulers and their short-eared slaves. The statues, resembling the Long Ears, are as tall as our mast and as heavy as a train. According to experts, the Short Ears chiseled them out of a mountainside known as "the factory" and dragged great numbers of them across the countryside to the coast, where they erected them on huge stone terraces. One day the work stopped and the adzes fell silent. The Short Ears eventually won the ensuing civil war and toppled the hated stone figures. The ones standing today were righted by the Chilean government to encourage tourism.

The whole hillside beneath the factory is covered with statues, some standing and some lying in the tall grass. These consisted only of a head, and, unlike the others by the road, each one was different. Asked what came to mind when they saw them, Tommy, Lisa and Doris replied, "Majestic, sad, lonely, forlorn, quiet, and mysterious." Here, at least, time seemed to have stood still.

Today, there are only a few descendants of the Long Ears, and the population of Easter Island is about 2,100. Planes make the flight from Santiago, Chile, every Wednesday. Juan Teave Haoa has a nice, clean boarding house with rooms at $12 a night, which includes breakfast. There is also a modern hotel.

Pitcairn Island, 1,200 miles from Easter Island, was downwind most of the way, although we did have a northwest gale for 12 hours.

During my watch on the evening we arrived at Pitcairn, the fan belt came off the engine pulley, causing the engine to overheat. Apparently I had not installed it properly the day before when I was servicing the alternator. We were lucky the engine was not damaged. There was enough breeze to keep the sails full while I fixed it, but the incident reminded us how much we relied on the engine. Not only could it push us at 4 knots on only a half-gallon of diesel an hour but it also provided us with electricity. This reliance on the engine is a necessary evil when you have a schedule to keep.

I had visited Pitcairn years earlier when the USCG *Eastwind* called there in 1961, and some people still remembered the visit because Irving Johnson's famous schooner *Yankee* was there at the same time.

There are only about 45 Pitcairn Islanders left, and 10 visitors. In 1936, there were 200. Many Easter Islanders had told us they were concerned about the rumor that the last Pitcairn people would be taken off the island because there weren't enough men to operate the lifeboats. I suppose the people of Easter Island, being similarly isolated on their own little rock, feel a kinship toward the people of Pitcairn.

In 1790, Fletcher Christian landed on Pitcairn with nine mutineers, six Tahitian men, and 12 Tahitian women after he seized the *Bounty*. He then sank the ship in Bounty Bay so that their presence would not be detected. The men fought over the women, and by 1800, John Adams was the sole male survivor. He was there until 1814, when an American ship rediscovered the island. By then there were 10 Polynesian women and 23 children. It was considered an act of great cruelty and inhumanity to arrest Adams for mutiny after 25 years, so he was allowed to live out the rest of his days on Pitcairn. In March 1831, the islanders all left for Tahiti, but they had little immunity to infectious diseases, and illness soon took its toll. Fletcher Christian's son died first, and 10 others died within two months. In September 1831, the survivors returned to Pitcairn. They had never felt at home in Tahiti, primarily because their sexual mores had become stricter than those of their hosts. In 1914, the opening of the Panama Canal placed Pitcairn on the direct route for passenger ships sailing to New Zealand and Australia. Some ships stopped briefly at Pitcairn Island and islanders went aboard to sell fruit and crafts. No longer

(above) Appledore *crew coming ashore, Easter Island. (below) Tom and statues, Easter Island.*

Herb, Tom and Lisa at
Pitcairn Island landing.

was Pitcairn Island isolated from the rest of the world. The island flag has always been a British Union Jack with a Bible and a wheelbarrow in yellow.

At Pitcairn, it was too dangerous to use our little skiff in the surf, so the islanders came out to get us in their 40-foot double-ended, diesel-powered aluminum launch. They duck behind a small jetty in Bounty Bay just after coming through the surf, and the ride is exciting. They hold the launch off, waiting for the right wave, and then slam the throttle full ahead. Doris looked at me worriedly, "Why are all the men yelling? Are they just having fun or are they as scared as I am?" The wave they had elected to take in was at least 5 feet, but it was no problem for these experienced seamen.

Doris, the kids, and I spent half a day walking around the island. Almost everyone is named Christian, Young, Adams, or Warren. We met Andrew Young, the oldest islander at 88, and Millie Christian, 84. Millie took us first to see the anchor, ship's bell and Bible from the *Bounty* and

Pitcairn Islanders climb aboard visiting freighter to trade.

then to her son-in-law's house, where she gave us cold drinks and showed us the new nine-bedroom house they were building. We also met a couple from Oregon who had been married on the island. Their wedding bands were made of copper that had come from the *Bounty*. The husband had been on the island 14 months. His wife, who had stayed in the United States to finish chemotherapy treatment for cancer, had arrived later. Outsiders can come to stay on the island, but they are screened very carefully and must be independently wealthy.

All the names of prominent points on Pitcairn have stories behind them. "Bang on Iron" was where the mutineers set up a forge. "Johnie Fall" is where John Mills fell from a cliff while gathering bird eggs in 1814. "Rachel's Coconut" is where Rachel Adams was born in 1791. "Howland Fall" is where Howland Christian fell from a line in 1884 while searching for bird eggs with his two brothers. "Where Minnie Off" rocks is where young Minnie Christian was washed off and almost drowned.

It was interesting that Pitcairn was dry for the locals but outsiders could obtain a license to drink alcoholic beverages. This is very different from many other islands, including Easter Island, where alcoholism is a major problem.

A surveyor who had been sent by the British government several months earlier was very pessimistic about the island. He told us he thought the people eventually would have to leave. New Zealand, he said, was too great an attraction for the young.

The community may survive perhaps for no other reason than its revenue. From 1980 to 1981, they sold more than $800,000 worth of stamps, which cost $340,000 to produce. They have done this for a number of years and invested their profits. The Seventh-Day Adventist Church has served the island for 90 years, and there is a school for children ages 5 to 15. There is no doctor, so for emergencies they have to flag down a passing ship and take the patient to Mangareva, 300 miles away, from where the sick person is flown to Tahiti. Just such an emergency occurred in 1984, when a small girl's appendix burst. A ship came within two days, and islanders took her out to it during a storm. In 24 hours, she was on the plane at Mangareva, was flown to Tahiti, and survived. In 1972, 48 ships called, but in 1985 only 23 ships arrived. Several of the islanders were somewhat angry that some ships swing in close to take a look but never establish contact with the island.

We were invited to stay overnight with families on the island. I knew I could not leave the boat because there is no anchorage at Pitcairn, but our entire crew did go ashore. Doris and I volunteered to take their watches. On May 1, we hove-to off Bounty Bay and the crew rejoined us. They had been ashore for only 18 hours, but that was enough. When we first saw Pitcairn two days earlier, some had wanted to skip the island altogether. Those same crew members now had a different appreciation for Pitcairn and said it had been the best stop so far. The people of Pitcairn are especially friendly, and they reprovisioned *Appledore* with bananas and other fresh fruits. Some even came on board to bid us farewell.

On the way to Tahiti, we had to change course slightly to keep out of the restricted French nuclear testing zone around Morane Atoll. The area covers 200 kilometers. We went 20 kilometers inside the zone, but I figured they would send out a surveillance plane with radar if they were about to test a bomb. Ironically, it was not something to take lightly. A few days after we arrived in Tahiti, the newspapers reported that a nuclear test had been conducted at Morane Atoll a week earlier. We must have missed it by days.

From Doris's log:

The passage from Pitcairn to Tahiti was a delightful sail with a following wind. These conditions help in the galley, and some meals were memorable, despite the fact that most of the ingredients were canned. Chicken and rice, three vegetables, and banana cream pie for dessert. Danish ham and scalloped potatoes with chocolate cake. Easter Island sweet potatoes, beef potpies, strained tomatoes, sliced pineapples, and banana bread. Still we missed fresh beef. At sea, Lisa did her best with her plate on the floor, since most of her food would end up there anyway. She never could remember that the table was not stationary. I had my meal in the cockpit with Herb, since dinner was always on his watch. More often than not, Lisa and Tommy would join us.

Tahiti is approximately 13,000 miles from Boothbay Harbor, Maine, if you sail around South America as we did. At dawn on May 11, we made the turn around Venus Point on the north coast of Tahiti and set our course for Papeete Harbor. My eyes scanned the western horizon for Moorea Island as I looked for something I had seen on three previous occasions. There it was — Bali Ha'i, a mountain jewel silhouetted in the morning sky and made famous by James A. Michener's *Tales of the South Pacific*. May 11 was also a good day to be getting in, because the following day was Mother's Day, and if we had been at sea, it would have been Doris's day to cook, and of course I would have had to take it instead. Furthermore, one year from that day, at 1:30 p.m., we would be sailing back into Boothbay Harbor.

It had taken us just 11 days to sail from Pitcairn to Tahiti, and after sailing 5,000 miles from Chile, with only a few short stops at remote islands, we all eagerly looked forward to this stop. We proceeded into the inner harbor under an unusually clear sky. The tops of Orofenua and Aorai mountains were visible. Tommy and Lisa were excited, partly because I had promised them ice cream cones for breakfast on shore. Lisa wanted hers with butterscotch and strawberries. Soon we were tied up to the customs dock and I went ashore to clear. After the ice cream, our next priority was the mail. It had been three months since our last mail stop.

Tahiti still exudes the romantic aura of the old sailing days. Dominated by the towering peaks of Orofenua (7,337 feet) and Aorai (6,786 feet), it is a beautiful and luxuriant island. Approximately 200 yachts were in transit here, although not all in Papeete, the capital. Some were scattered around the island in different lagoons. French Polynesia has a unique culture. Although Papeete is modern, with all of the conveniences of any small American city, a nineteenth-century tradition still survives a short distance outside the city limits. The men still fish the reefs with canoes, and some families still live in thatched houses, which they claim to be the coolest type of tropical dwelling. The women weave baskets and wrap a single piece of cloth called a *pareu* around their bodies. They have wonderful smiles and love to laugh. Polynesians are noted for their hospitality, friendliness, and easygoing approach to life, so Tahiti is the pearl in the oyster shell for world voyagers. Yachts *Star Chaser, Wave*

Aboard icebreaker Eastwind, *off Tahiti.*

Dancer, Enchantress, Galaxy, Wandering Star, Moonraker, Sundancer, and *Appledore* were all here at the same time, and the crews exchanged stories of adventures on the high seas. Lin and Larry Pardey, associate editors for *Sail* magazine, visited aboard *Appledore* during our stay here.

Our original crew of five was still with us and had no plans to give it up, except for Ray, who would be replaced by his daughter in Cape Town. They deserved a lot of credit for their fortitude. Some had not realized that going around South America and through the Strait of Magellan would present a special sailing challenge. All five were doing fine, and they did a good job of sharing the work of sailing. At sea, each took a four-hour daily turn at the wheel and one day of cooking per week. In port, we each spent one day out of six watching *Appledore,* making the launch runs, cooking, and doing routine maintenance.

On all of our trips, it has been interesting to observe our crew members' expectations of port life. A few of the older crew members tended to want to meet and get to know someone closely, to stay in their homes and to eat with them. Others stuck to the usual tourist paths. They were content to be observers, barely touching elbows with the local people and preferring to meet crew members from other yachts.

With so many young people on board, we could not help but be concerned while they were ashore. Doris and I kept reminding ourselves that if their parents had not thought them mature enough to handle their own lives, they would not be with us. Although there still is a tendency to want to set limits, we guarded ourselves carefully from doing that. They came on board as adults and they had to make their own mistakes. I offered a few opinions about staying safe and out of trouble, but the last thing they wanted was a lecture.

In Tahiti, Doris and I divided our time between filming and the maintenance of *Appledore*, including hauling her out to scrub and paint the bottom, which took two days. Considering where we had been and how many miles we had covered, she did not look bad. With help from Chris and Bob, the job went along quite quickly.

Our stay in Tahiti lasted three weeks, including a four-day trip to Moorea Island, 16 miles away, where on our last voyage we had visited with Bernard Moitessier (a well known French author and seaman). He lived in a small house a short distance up from the water and was contentedly working in a garden. Later he came on board *Appledore* for an inspection and we visited his steel ketch *Joshua*. This time he was not around and we wondered what had happened to him. While in Tahiti we sent our Magnavox satellite navigator back to the factory in California for repairs, and they quickly sent us a new one free of charge. I had been a bit skeptical about purchasing it, but I must admit that it was a good decision. If there is no engine to charge a 12-volt battery, which the satellite navigator requires, it can be maintained with a small wind generator or solar panel, since the draw on the battery is not very much. Originally, the major drawback of a satellite navigator was its cost of $10,000 or more to install. Now they are down to $2,000 and take only minutes to install. The U.S. government has sent up several satellites that are on polar orbits at altitudes of 620 miles. They circle the earth every 107 minutes. Twenty years ago, they were used solely by the armed forces and probably were top secret. Now they are used commercially by all ships at sea. Our Magnavox MX 4102 tracks five different satellites. When one of them passes overhead, it sends a signal for approximately 15 minutes. During this time, the satellite navigator calculates our position and displays our position in latitude and longitude to within a couple of hundred feet. It does not always give us a position, however, since the satellite that it is tracking has to be not higher than 70° or lower than 7° above the horizon. The longest that I have seen it go without updating our position is eight hours, but you cannot do any better using a sextant to shoot the stars.

This system will be vastly improved in the next five years, and our unit probably will be obsolete. The next system, to be called Global Positioning System, will employ up to 18 satellites to provide continuous

Appledore *anchored*
off Moorea.

satellite positioning 24 hours a day. Deer hunters in the woods will have a
pocket-sized Sat-Nav to pinpoint their locations, and surveyors also will
be using them. The Sat-Nav, however, will never tell you where to go; it
only tells you where you are — and if you are not careful, that may be on
top of a reef. You can never become too relaxed about navigating and
always must plot your positions carefully. Furthermore, all electronic
equipment will malfunction. You need back ups.

Provisions are three times more expensive in Tahiti than in the United
States, so we did not plan to resupply there. We would wait until arriving
at American Samoa, only three weeks away. May is Tahiti's autumn, and
this one was particularly wet. We often would be walking through inches
of warm rain, only to be dried out moments later by a steaming-hot sun.
We visited the Paul Gauguin museum and went to numerous dance shows
that were reenactments of Tahiti's past. Each evening we returned to the

Church, Tahiti.

boat worn out with fatigue, only to fall asleep on deck beneath the stars. We had captured it all on 5,000 feet of motion- picture film.

On June 3, 1985, we departed Tahiti for American Samoa, just 1,200 miles downwind. At night in this latitude, we could see the Big Dipper in the northern sky, reminding us of the Northern Hemisphere and home.

Just 80 miles from American Samoa, we came across a school of tuna, and everyone who wanted to catch one did. At one point, there was a tuna on each line. We kept the smaller, 10-pound yellowfin and released the bluefin. We had plenty to eat.

We arrived at American Samoa at 6:00 a.m. on June 15. A few hours before our arrival, our view of the island had been obscured by poor visibility and heavy rain. After tying up, I learned that Saturday was a holiday. Besides port fees, we would have to pay overtime customs and immigration fees if we wanted to go ashore. Or we could wait until Monday and not have to pay the overtime. With only five days scheduled there, I paid. While we were in Samoa, Donald Hodel, the U.S. secretary of the interior, who administers the island's affairs in Washington, was visiting, and there was quite a celebration. All the local dancers were performing for him in full native dress, and he received many gifts, including a large roasted pig. The local people had worked hard, cleaning up the island and sprucing up the major town of Pago Pago with new paint. It was all being broadcast on the South Pacific's first television station. Samoa now had three stations. It was strange being back in United States territory halfway through our voyage and in the middle of the Pacific Ocean. We even indulged in some television on Tommy's computer monitor.

Samoa also has two large department stores and many large grocery stores, so we restocked with more than 50 cases of food. The cost was only slightly higher than it would have been back home. For any yacht cruising the South Pacific, it is well worth resupplying in American Samoa. We also received mail and duty-free packages there.

While in Samoa, we had time to tour the Star-Kist tuna factory, which employs more than a thousand people. The tuna are frozen and stored in large refrigerators. When ready to can, they are washed, cleaned, and thawed, and placed in 30-foot walk-through ovens. After cooking, they go by conveyor belt to a huge building about the size of a modern college gymnasium. On both sides of the conveyor belt, hundreds of women dressed in white uniforms and hairnets pick and grade the tuna. Some parts are used for 9-Lives cat food and fertilizer; nothing is wasted. The tuna then goes into the can and is packed in either oil or spring water. This factory puts up 5,000 cases of tuna a day, a total of 240,000 cans. We purchased two 48-can cases of chunk white tuna in spring water for $77.

We were sad to see that the Coast Guard was no longer here. On our first voyage, our anchor had somehow been dropped without the shackle being wired, and it was not long before I noticed we were drifting. Two off-duty Coast Guardsmen came over to help us locate it. Using a grappling hook, we miraculously snagged the anchor, located in 100 feet of water. We had sent a diver down, but the water was so dark and murky, he couldn't see anything.

A lot of other things had changed in Pago Pago since our first visit. The Rainmaker Hotel, which had been demolished by a plane crash, had been rebuilt. Gone, however, was the cable car up to a mountain overlooking the bay. Gone, too, were the 40 or 50 Korean fishing boats that used to be moored in the harbor waiting to unload or get hauled out on the government ways. In their place was the super-modern and highly expensive American tuna fleet. The government railway where we had hauled *Appledore II* had been sold to a private firm, which had rebuilt it and was opening it to the tuna fleet the week we were there. Time flies in port, and five days was not long enough to do much sightseeing. Purchasing food supplies and fresh vegetables, mailing film, changing engine oil, getting diesel fuel delivered to the boat, doing the laundry, clearing immigration and customs took most of the five days, and we departed on June 19.

Dancer, Fiji.

It is only 750 miles from American Samoa to Fiji, but there are many islands and reefs en route, including the Tonga Islands and the Eastern Fiji Island group. We saw lots of islands on the horizon and got close enough to a couple of them to see surf breaking on the beaches. On all of our passages, we would see lightning almost every night, and this passage was no exception. These lightning storms, I believe, represent the greatest hazard to yachts at sea. They perhaps are the mystery behind the Bermuda Triangle. We keep our fingers crossed. When you are the only object standing above the surface of the water for miles, you feel very vulnerable.

It was no longer possible to start a passage with a refrigerator full of fresh meat. It would go bad within days unless we kept it frozen, but now that we were in the tradewinds, we were not using the engine to charge the batteries. Although we had taken on some excellent canned food in Boothbay Harbor, that could never satisfy our craving for fresh foods.

We were visited one afternoon on this passage by 25-foot pilot whales, which swam beside us for a half hour. The spray from their blowholes even got on our camera lenses. They came so close that Lisa and Tommy could have touched them, and at times I thought I felt them nudge the side of the hull. Doris and I were a little disappointed that we had not seen more whales on this trip. Maybe it was the different route we had taken to the Pacific, but it seemed we were seeing fewer of them than on the first trip.

We approached Fiji at 1:00 a.m. on June 26. I slowed down to go in at daybreak, because these South Pacific islands are often fringed with coral reefs, and Fiji is no exception, although Suva, the capital, has a modern harbor with range lights and lighted buoys. As we got closer, I was able to pick out the lights, and we sailed into the harbor at 3:00 a.m. We dropped anchor across from the main dock in the quarantine area indicated on the chart and hoisted our yellow quarantine flag to show the officials that we had just arrived from a foreign country. We could see the city in the glow of the many streetlights, and modern high-rise buildings lined the waterfront. What captured my attention most, however, was the strong, pleasant smell of coconut oil emerging from the soap factory across the street. This triggered a nostalgic memory of the first time I had come to Fiji, 25 years earlier, as a bosun's mate aboard the icebreaker *Eastwind*.

At 8:15 a.m., the harbor launch came alongside and an officer from the health department came aboard. I had to fill out the usual papers, which took about 15 minutes, and answer the usual questions. "No, there is no one on board with an infectious disease and there were no births or deaths while at sea." He then gave us our first clearance. Next we had to take the boat alongside the customs dock, where I filled out more papers and provided them with two lists of all the crew members' names and addresses. Having done this, I had to report to the agriculture office and fill out some papers stating what we had on board for food supplies. This was quite time-consuming because we had more than 200 cases of canned food, plus fresh oranges, potatoes, vegetables, and rice. They also wanted to know what country all of the food had come from.

Next I had to go back to the customs office and accompany the customs officer back to *Appledore*, where he would do an inspection. He took down the serial numbers of our rifle and shotgun. Later, I had to turn these weapons in to the authorities for safekeeping while we were visiting Fiji.

The immigration officials arrived, and each crew member had to fill out a form that included name, address, date of birth, passport number, and so on. The agriculture officer came aboard for his inspection and asked if we had any pets. "Well, sort of, if you want to call it that," I said. I asked Doris to get our hamster and show it to them. Hampie fascinated them. I doubt they have seen many hamsters. I had to admit it did look like a mouse, but they could see it was a friendly and unusual mouse, since Tommy was holding it. However, this meant another form to fill out, and an officer had to go back to the office to get it. I had to post a bond stating that the hamster would remain on board at all times. I told

Doris to be sure the cage was taped shut, because if Hampie got loose, as he had in the past, it would cost us $500.

We had just about completed all of the paperwork and inspections for a routine clearing-in process, but then there was one more detail. I had to take the clearances from the health, customs, and immigration to building number four, the harbormaster's office, to pay our port fees. I had done it a hundred times before, and there is nothing to it. In fact, while the crew was quarantined on board, I, as the captain, was able to move around with freedom. The officials were always friendly, happy to have us visit their country.

After we cleared, everyone was allowed ashore, and since Doris and I had the first duty day in Suva, the rest of the crew quickly disappeared. We decided to anchor a short distance from the city in the Bay of Islands, in front of the Tradewinds Hotel, where we had been made most welcome on our last voyage. Using the chart, I showed everyone where we would be when they came back to the boat that night.

A routine first day in port consisted of going to the market and this time we went for fresh vegetables, bread, and cheese. Then I went to the Australian and New Guinea embassies to apply for visas. Now a problem arose, because each embassy would need to keep the passports for three working days and wanted a photograph of each crew member. Since we were only staying for five days and two of them were over the weekend, the Australian Embassy said it was impossible to process visas. Now that's a word that triggers an automatic response from me. "Why is it impossible? I have the passports with me and I will be back with the photos in a moment."

Suva is a big city, but I found two of our crew members and told them we needed photos, and they found the others. When I got back to the Australian Embassy at 12:30, it was closed for the day, so I rushed over to the New Guinea Embassy, where I was able to get the forms that needed to be filled out and signed by each crew member. When everyone returned to the schooner, we got organized. For the next two days, Doris, the kids, and I shuffled passports back and forth between embassies and managed to get all the visas for our next ports of call.

We soon discovered that most of the yachts no longer anchored in front of the Tradewinds Hotel. The new management felt that visiting yachtsmen were too demanding. After a drug raid on several of the yachts a week earlier, all of them had been kicked out of the basin. I certainly could understand their feelings. I talked to the management and they agreed to let us stay, but the atmosphere was not the same. Most of the yachts now anchored in front of the Suva Yacht Club.

Port Villa, Vanuatu.

Suva is a fascinating place to visit, with a diversified population. When sugar cane became a major crop on the island, people were brought from India to work on the plantations. Now the Indian population has surpassed that of the native Fijians. Since this was the first time we had come in contact with either the Fijian or the Indian culture, we found their customs and dress very interesting. Many of the Indian women still dress in the traditional sari, and native Fijian men dress in suits, of which the bottom half consists of a *lavalava* (skirt) rather than Western-style pants.

We visited the cultural center, which had an interesting display of a traditional Fijian village with battlements and buildings built without nails. Everything was lashed together with vine and rope. The lashings were not only supportive but also decorative. We went on a ride in a *takia*, an outrigger canoe, and were taken on a tour of the village, which featured traditional Fijian arts and crafts. Our tour guide was exceptional. It was refreshing to see someone so obviously interested in and proud of his heritage. He transported us into the past, when Fiji had a cannibalistic society and was unaffected by Western civilization. The day ended with an excellent dancing exhibition.

We also visited a dairy farm boasting 130 holsteins. Since I have considered a dairy business myself, I was particularly interested in their operations. Their average cow produces only 25 pounds of milk a day, compared to the U.S. holstein average of approximately 55 pounds. It may be due mostly to the feed. Fijian cows are fed coconut milk, molasses, bran fiber from the local brewery, and hay. They don't have high-quality hay or productive cows.

Webb Chiles, author of *Storm Passage* and many other nautical books, came aboard in Suva and we exchanged yarns. He is now sailing the South Pacific with a 40-foot fiberglass boat and a female companion. Meeting interesting people like Webb is an additional bonus when sailing around the world.

On Monday, July 1, after we all had cholera shots at the Red Cross Clinic, I went through the same routine as on the first day with customs, immigration and so forth, but in reverse. We departed at 1:30 p.m. for Port Vila, Vanuatu. Finally, we were almost on schedule.

The weather was rather dismal when we left Fiji. In fact, we could not see across the harbor because of the rain, but there was a fair breeze from the southeast that we could not pass up. Two days later, that breeze increased to 45 knots, and we were in a full gale.

The gale came up from nowhere. We could only be thankful that it was not a hurricane. The barometer dropped only slightly as the wind roared in from the southeast. It was a fair wind, so we could hold our course, but we had to take down all but the small staysail forward. Still, we were making 7 knots, and by dusk, the seas were building to incredible heights, much higher than the wind called for. It must have been blowing a lot harder a short distance from our position, or else we had an opposing current. The waves would build up behind us and tower 30 feet above us, sometimes with the top 6 feet breaking. Our stern would rise and the bow would drop as the wave rushed by under the hull. A few times, part of a wave rolled over the stern and crashed on deck. We made the mistake of leaving our aft hatch open a couple of inches for air, and it took a wave. Tommy's computer monitor fell off the chart table, along with the hamster's cage, and landed right under the hatch just as the water poured in. The hamster survived but the monitor did not. During the night, the wind moderated. We all wore life harnesses to keep us on board should a wave sweep the decks. By midnight, the seas were smoothing out, and soon we hoisted more sail. We covered the 600 miles to Vanuatu, formerly the New Hebrides, in four days, arriving on July 6.

Vanuatu is now an independent nation, and proud of it. Port Vila was a pleasant surprise. It had grown a great deal since we had last visited in 1980. It was clean and modern and the people were friendly. Its beaches, as always, were beautifully white and virtually unused. It would be a great place to spend a leisurely vacation.

In the last three ports, I had been searching for the ingredients for planting vegetable seeds in some small plastic containers on deck. I had always believed this would be a great thing to do to supply fresh vegetables at sea. In the old days, they kept turtles and hens for fresh meat. On our previous trip, we had grown sprouts, but they had not been popular. No one wanted to take care of growing them, especially when we were in ports where we could buy lettuce and other vegetables. I had purchased organic fertilizer in Samoa, seeds in Fiji, and now I only needed some soil. I asked around for this, and in one shop, the Chinese proprietor said he could help us out. His name was Wai Tong Wong, and he said his father had a vegetable garden only two miles away. I was to meet him at 8:00 a.m. the next day in front of his shop.

I arrived at 8:00, and he was waiting in his car with his two small children. He took me to a plot of land high on a hilltop two miles away. Facing the southwest, I could see the blue Coral Sea stretching out to the horizon. It looked impressive. At Wai Tong Wong's homestead was a perfect one-acre vegetable garden. Cucumbers were hanging on a fence; peas were growing up their stalks; tomato plants were in neat rows; and lettuce, onions, and spinach were all planted in raised beds. Not a weed was in sight. Wai Tong pointed out that raised beds were commonplace in China, but that the people in Vanuatu planted everything flat. This being their winter, with a morning temperature of only 68°, the peas were doing fine. Everyone on the island was complaining about the cold and wearing extra-heavy clothing, even though the daytime temperature got up to 80°.

Wai Tong's cousin ran a Chinese restaurant beside the garden, and since it was Sunday morning and Wai Tong did not have to open his shop, he invited me to breakfast. He asked me what I would like and I said, "Oh, just some toast would be fine." But after we sat down, he said they had no bread in the restaurant, so he was going out to get some. I told him not to bother — I would have whatever he was having. Soon he placed in front of me something that looked like raw squid with pieces of shrimp mixed in. I found it hard to swallow, and, with his children wolfing it down and enjoying it, I felt a little uneasy. I was relieved when Wai Tong said he was going to get something else and asked if I was finished. Next came a bowl of soup that tasted like . . . well, let me say that I just could not eat it, and I became even more uneasy. It was a good cultural exchange. After breakfast, I took his family out to visit *Appledore* and gave them a copy of *Dreams of Natural Places*. They didn't stay on board long, however, because they felt seasick.

In the afternoon, I planted the lettuce and radish seeds in three plastic containers, and the next day, July 8, after buying our last hamburger at Bloody Mary's ("Fast Foods in Paradise,"), we departed for

Papua New Guinea.

It is 1,300 miles from Port Vila to Port Moresby, New Guinea, a direct run with no obstacles in between. Now in the Coral Sea with a fair southeast breeze, we got back into the routine of passing time at sea. Tommy and Lisa did their Calvert School lessons. Tommy had completed 154 of his 160 second-grade lessons. Lisa was doing an occasional kindergarten lesson, but we never went far with her course since she didn't seem to be ready for it. Nor were we ready to devote the time and patience needed to make it meaningful. The last thing we wanted to do was to give her a negative attitude toward learning. She would just be starting school when we returned home.

Day Allen baked some brownies and did some writing. Ray Corbett wrote letters and notes and identified the white-bellied storm petrels that swooped down and hit their breasts on the water. These unusual creatues act as though there is something wrong with them. Kate Harris kept busy reading and writing and baking bread. Chris Merriam worked on the political science course that he sent into Bowling Green State University for college credits. He had to write a paper on his observations of each port that we visited. He also caught a 30-pound fish. Bob Royal did some reading and, like Chris, some fishing. He caught a large tuna that got away just as he was about to bring it aboard. I just daydreamed and schemed toward other goals. I had mentioned that it might be nice to get a monkey and become an organ grinder. Doris looked at me as if to say, "You have been out in the sun too long." The biggest obsession I had, though, was with dairy cows. Tommy and I planned the perfect farm. At sea farming looks good. Back on land farming is boring and one yearns for another sea adventure.

On the third day at sea, the wind died, and we were making 4 knots using the engine. At night, we had some serious thunder and lightning just five or six miles to our north. By the sixth day, however, the wind came back and my seeds were sprouting. We had to keep them covered at night in case we had a downpour. They got plenty of sunlight during the day. What a pleasure it was to see them grow, since the surface of the sea is so empty of noticeable life. By the end of that passage, the lettuce had four leaves and Tommy and Lisa were taking a keen interest in watching it grow. We had also picked up a cricket that chirped each night from the forward chain box. It was like a summer evening ashore. But we had more. We were on the move.

We were on a broad reach practically all the way to New Guinea, except for the three calm days, with a wind of 15 to 20 knots and a smooth sea. It was a great passage. We arrived on July 18, just before dark.

Port Moresby, New Guinea.

New Guinea to Darwin

Papua New Guinea is considered a Third World country. It is also the third largest producer of gold in the world, and, unlike most Third World countries, its trade budget is balanced. In the city of Port Moresby are large grocery stores with computer checkouts, a large department store similar to Sears, a deluxe 12-story hotel, and many other modern facilities.

In the hills of Papua New Guinea, things are quite different. There, tribes are still fighting, mostly over boundary lines, and the women are still having 10 children each to increase the size of the tribe and gain more power. The infant mortality rate has decreased dramatically, and now Papua New Guinea's population doubles every 20 years.

The tribal wars are still fought with primitive spears and bows and arrows. Two weeks prior to our arrival, a group of tourists went up to visit one of the highland tribes that was doing battle with another tribe. The tourists asked one of the chiefs if they could cross the war zone to get a better vantage point. The two sides agreed, the tourists drove to the other side unharmed, and the battle resumed.

In Port Moresby, we were tied up alongside Ernie Lohberger's boat (we had met Ernie on our first voyage five years earlier). The Royal Port Moresby Yacht Club graciously extended us honorary membership. They have hot and cold running showers, something that we had not experienced since Mar del Plata six months earlier. The yacht basin was modernized in 1980, but there still was not enough water for a comfortable stay. At low tide, we grounded out on a ledge. With our full-length iron keel, we sustained no damage, but it scared some of the crew when they looked out the yacht club windows and saw *Appledore* pitching forward. Chris ran down to the boat, thinking she was sinking, and pulled up the floorboards. When he saw no water in the bilge, he realized that she was aground. The boat we were rafted up to had a shallower draft and had remained afloat. Chris was a conscientious crew member and helpful on many occasions.

Ernie Lohberger was the Ford parts distributor in Papua New Guinea, and since most of the Ford diesels that he serviced were used as generators in the outlying villages, he entertained us one evening with tales about the outback. He told us of a friend who owned a general store that was held up by two men with bows and arrows. The owner resisted and was hit in the shoulder and stomach with arrows. The lower one pierced his liver, and he was evacuated to Australia, where he finally recovered. He returned to his store but was apprehensive about staying there, until the chief came by to inform him that he need never again worry about those two men. I asked Ernie what happened to them, and he said, "No one will ever know. They're just not around anymore." The tribe had taken care of them because the store owner was well liked and the tribe wanted the store to remain in the village. They have an odd system of retribution. More than one foreigner has been whisked quickly out of New Guinea after a car accident in which a native had been hurt.

I did some filming in the city, where red stains dot the sidewalks. People chew betelnuts, a mild stimulant and narcotic, and spit out its red juice. Chewing the nut, along with lime to get rid of the bitter taste, has greatly raised the incidence of mouth cancer. All of my pictures of the local people come complete with wide smiles and a mouthful of red teeth.

Because of small local problems with the criminal element of their society, the government here had instituted a very strict 10:00 p.m. curfew. The situation seemed to be getting better, so there was talk that it would be lifted shortly. Many people, however, liked the curfew, and they said they could sleep all night for the first time without hearing barking dogs. It was quiet after 10:00 p.m. If you did need to go out, you could get a special pass, but if you had none, there was an automatic $500 fine. One night, a couple of our shipmates had to stay in a motel because they could not make it back to the boat in time. Doris had wanted to go up into the highlands, but until we knew the extent of the tribal problems, we had not dared go, especially with the children. By the time we discovered it was safe, we had to leave for Australia. Schedules have their disadvantages.

We sailed from Papua New Guinea on July 21, carrying eight frozen chickens and 41 pounds of ground steak in our small freezer. This would help the morale on our 12-day passage to Darwin. I make this comment to enlighten those who have been conditioned by glamorous sailing magazine advertisements to believe that sailing is all pleasure. In my opinion, it's not for everyone, and it is wise to experience an offshore passage before investing. A lot of sacrifices need to be made in the creature-comfort department. For me, the rewards are the new goals that lie ahead: completing a passage, getting to the next port safely, meeting new and interesting people, observing new cultures, sharing in others' dreams. What makes the voyage more interesting is that every passage between ports is a goal in itself. That probably is why I have looked forward to getting back to sea so often.

Before reaching Darwin, we had to find the reef-fringed entrance to the Torres Strait, marked by Bramble Cay, a small, sandy island 10 feet high. There was an additional danger at the beginning of this passage — huge floating logs had been washed down from New Guinea streams during the northwest monsoon and blown out to sea. The wind had shifted to the prevailing southeast summer winds, and the logs and trees were being blown back toward shore. We saw many logs, some with birds roosting on them. Two yachts had serious encounters with these logs, and one sank in eight minutes, but all hands were saved by the Australian navy. The other vessel escaped serious damage.

As we approached Bramble Cay, the wind was steady at 25 knots and the seas were running about 8 to 10 feet. At dusk, 14 birds landed aloft on the springstay and along the lifelines. They made some unusually sloppy landings and one even landed on Bob's shoulder. Apparently liking what they saw, they decided to stay the night. They were so tame that we could walk right up to them. At dawn, they flew off, leaving their marks on the deck and sails. They returned the next evening, but we were determined not to let them roost again. We had spent much of the day cleaning up their droppings. A check in our bird book indicated they had been boobies.

During the night, our Sat-Nav did not give us many positions and ironically, no usable satellites were scheduled in the morning. We never did see Bramble Cay, because we entered Torres Strait 12 miles to the south. On our last voyage, we used only sextants, and Bramble Cay came up dead ahead. Twelve miles off was not too bad. It is surprising how many yachts miss large islands completely. If it is overcast and you cannot get sights, it is sheer luck. One yachtsman told me he missed his landfall by 125 miles, and in the old days along our New England coast, Boon Island Light often was mistaken for Boston Light by fishing schooners returning from the Grand Banks — a miss of 60 miles.

Once into Torres Strait, we were behind the Great Barrier Reef, and although the sea became smooth, the wind increased. We reefed the mainsail and started passing small islands. A few shrimp boats were in the channels. Late in the day, we were getting some heavy squalls with 40 knots of wind and plenty of rain, so we dropped anchor behind Rennel Island. Some shrimp boats anchored there had female crew members who looked like roller- derby players. We were in the lee, and the reefs broke the long Pacific swells so, it was comfortable. We decided to stay the next day, and everyone went ashore on this uninhabited island, where we could swim on a lovely sandy beach and find shade under coconut trees. Doris found some unbroken nautilus shells to add to her large shell collection.

Late in the evening, the weather improved and the sky was full of bright stars. Listening to Australian radio stations, we felt a long way from home. Rennel Island had been an unexpected pleasure. We had not been able to stop at many uninhabited beaches on this trip, but after one day of idleness, everyone was anxious to get to Australia.

At 1:00 a.m., we got underway, this would give us the most daylight hours for navigating the most difficult part of the strait. The lights were all working in the channel, and we passed Dove Island at 5:30 a.m. By noon, we had only 40 miles to go to be clear of Torres Strait. Along the way, we passed a large ship aground that had failed to make a right-angle turn. It had been lying on its side there for many years. Doris used the leftover spaghetti sauce to make pizza for lunch, and we enjoyed a beautiful calm, sunny day of sailing. By 5:00 p.m., we had passed Booby Island and were in the Arafura Sea, only 600 miles from Darwin. This was an exciting point, since in my mind we were now homeward bound; there was no turning back.

During the next few days, Tommy finished his second-grade course and plotted all our positions from the Sat-Nav. Day baked bread, Chris cooked a great chicken dinner, Bob cooked his by-now-famous corned-beef-hash dish, Kate baked cherry squares, and I cooked popcorn. We had gone through 80 pounds of popcorn and were running low.

The garden we had started was finished. The radishes did not do well, but the lettuce had come along. The experiment turned out to be somewhat impractical because the plants had to be covered when we took any spray or heavy rain, and they required a lot of fresh water, something we did not have in abundance. We fed the lettuce to the hamster. In Australia, the plants would have had to be destroyed because of very strict quarantine regulations — all vegetables, eggs, and fresh meats must be disposed of before arrival.

We arrived in Darwin on July 30, at 4:00 p.m., and customs, immigration, and health cleared us. We had to seal many things on board with customs tags. Popcorn was one of them. By dusk, we were anchored a mile off the Darwin Sailing Club in 12 feet of water. The tide rises and falls 25 feet here, which made for a long skiff run to shore, but the holding was great in beach sand.

A new problem has beset Darwin Harbor — vicious saltwater crocodiles. A recent ban on killing them has caused them to multiply. A woman in a canoe was attacked and just barely got away, later spending months in a hospital. Other boats suffered attacks such as shown in the

Appledore *off Fatu Hiva, Marquesas.*

Tom visits Paul Gauguin's grave, Hiva Oa.

(right) Market woman with child, Fiji. (below) Hauled out at Darwin, Australia.

Country people, Bali.

Men in the village of Cilaos, Reunion. (below) Market at Port Louis, Mauritius.

(above) Point Yacht Club, Durban. (below) Cape Town and Table Mountain.

Elephants, Kruger National Park.

Why does a fish have wings?

St. Helena

(above) Tom and a friend, Barbados. (below) Appledore III returns to Boothbay Harbor, Maine to cheers of friends and family. Photo by Peter E. Randall.

Katharine Gorge, Australia.

movie *Jaws* — but from crocodiles instead of sharks. As we waded out
with the skiff the last quarter-mile in knee-deep water at low tide, we were
not very comfortable. With every pothole Doris slipped into, she was sure a
croc had gotten her. Later in our stay, we would visit a croc farm, where
they not only raised crocs for their skins but also incarcerated the
environmental problems. One of them was 16 feet long. We were amazed at
how fast they were — no human could outrun one of them if they had to.

In Darwin, Doris and I and the kids spent our first night ashore (On
our first world voyage we never did spent a night ashore). *Appledore* was
anchored well and our shipmates now were experienced enough for us to
feel comfortable leaving the boat. We rented a car and drove inland 160
miles to Katherine Gorge. The scenery across Australia's Northern
Territory is flat and dry, with large, red termite mounds dotting the
landscape. Tractor-trailer trucks pulling five trailers, called road trains,
were a common sight. The weather was dry, clear, and hot, with no
rainfall. It's the complete opposite in January and February.

At Katherine Gorge, we took a small motorboat up one gorge, then
disembarked and hiked to the next one. After five hours, we were at the
fifth gorge, with magnificent scenery. People had warned us that we
might have to carry Lisa most of the way, because the large rocks would
prevent her from keeping up. They were right. While I carried the camera

equipment, Doris carried Lisa on her shoulders. Lisa got carried away and insisted on holding a piece of long grass that she whipped Doris with, yelling, "Come on, horsey, faster, faster." Tommy, embarrassed by all this, was at the front of the pack with the guides and the adults. It was well worth the effort, however, and a highlight of this voyage. Fortunately, they did not try to feed us Vegimite for lunch. A brownish salty paste they use for a sandwich spread, Vegimite is something you have to have grown up with to appreciate.

Back at the boat, everything was in order as we expected, and the next day we drove *Appledore* up on the beach at high tide and leaned her against some pilings. When the tide went out, we washed and painted the bottom. The hull was in good shape, but the opportunity for a fresh coat of paint was too good to pass up.

The kids particularly enjoyed the yacht club, which came complete with a playground and plenty of children to play with. Darwin was also a good port for stocking up on children's books. The children were amused by local road signs, such as "Wallaby Crossing."

We rarely saw the crew in Darwin. With a good exchange rate, motel rooms were very reasonable. It was cheaper for them to rent a room together than to pay for a taxi back to the yacht club every night.

On August 12, we left Darwin for Bali. Just a few miles outside Darwin Harbor, Kate spotted a boat waving a distress flag, so we changed course and investigated. They had run out of gas, and we were able to try our new radio antenna to call back their position to Darwin. Help would soon arrive.

On this passage, the sea was as calm and flat as a piece of glass. At night, the stars reflected in it, making it impossible to see where sea and sky met. We motored to Bali, 950 miles away, at 4.5 knots.

At 2:00 one morning, Day Allen reported that a ship was approaching. When I got up, I could see that we were on a collision course. I altered course a few degrees and called the ship on our radio. He said he was a shark-fishing boat out of Darwin and asked if we had any cigarettes. I had to tell him no one smoked so we couldn't help, but even if I had had a hundred packs, I would not have wanted to go alongside to pass them across. Although I recognized the boat as one I had seen in Darwin, his request was a typical ruse used by modern-day pirates.

On every passage, I manage to keep busy plotting positions, changing the engine lubricating oil, replacing light bulbs, fixing the toilet, watching the weather, or just observing the foam patterns peeling away from *Appledore's* hull. I spend a lot of time at this indulgence. The rest of the crew, including Doris and Tom, were insatiable readers. We finally had to put a limit on Tom's reading. We often found him still going at 3:00 a.m., and even after we prohibited him from reading beyond

9:00 p.m., he would sit in the hatch and talk to Chris or Kate on watch. I think he enjoyed these conversations almost as much as his reading. He especially liked to sit with Kate, who was a good listener.

Lisa generally spent her time in her swimming pool, which we had made by cutting off the top of a 50-gallon plastic juice container. We would all look at her enviously as she sat in cool water up to her neck, oblivious to the scorching heat that had the rest of us mopping our brows.

The calm weather continued, and at noon it was so hot on deck that we couldn't walk there with bare feet. With the engine running continuously below, we found relief only after the sun had dropped below the horizon. The engine kept the after cabin unbearably hot 24 hours a day. Remembering our first voyage, I had installed a couple of fans in that cabin. Without them, it would have been impossible to stay in our bunks. The engine heat would rise up behind the ceiling and drift into the two nearest berths.

During this passage, we saw many sea snakes. We circled one and tried to hook it for closer inspection but missed. That was probably just as well, since they are one of the most deadly things in the ocean.

On August 21, we entered Benoa Harbor, Bali, a stop that had required a year of negotiations and persistent efforts — including using an Indonesian government agent — to get a $260 sailing permit. It was supposed to be waiting for us with the navy commander in Bali. Just before departing from Darwin, I confirmed this by telegram to Jakarta, but it was a holiday when we arrived, and no one knew anything about our clearance. We would have to wait two days for the holiday period to end, and until then, we were not allowed to go ashore.

In two days, everything was straightened out. Our clearance was there and we spent 10 days sightseeing. Few cruising yachts were visiting Bali because of the hassle of getting a permit. The first time we had written to the agent, while we were building *Appledore,* they had replied that the Indonesian government was not issuing permits to American yachts because they suspected some of them of gun-running. Just before we were to leave the States, we had written again and were surprised to learn that they now were issuing permits. Not all of the agents were as honest as ours. Australian customs officials told us they knew of only two other yachts that had been able to secure the proper documents. Another yacht that arrived with engine problems and no permit paid $60 per week per person to be allowed to stay, even though only the captain was allowed ashore.

Bali, the most exotic place we would visit on this voyage, is a Hindu island in predominantly Muslim Indonesia. There were Hindu shrines and temples on every corner. Small offerings of rice and flowers littered the sidewalks for protection and luck from the Hindu gods and goddesses.

Rice farmer, Bali.

There was also an incredible mix of new and old here. You could take a horse-drawn cab to Kentucky Fried Chicken or an air-conditioned taxi to any of the ancient Hindu temples. At the markets, women carried produce on their heads. I noticed no dump trucks or other equipment that could do what people could do. With Bali's large population, everything was done by hand to give everyone work.

The countryside, which is dominated by rice paddies, is hilly. Farmers take advantage of this by terracing their fields so that water fed to the uppermost fields would irrigate the lower fields. As they have for centuries, harnessed water buffalos plow the fields and women harvest the rice by hand.

We hired a taxi driver named Wyan, meaning "number one son," to take care of our driving needs for the week. Tommy was impressed by his very long fingernails, a sign that he did no manual labor. I was impressed by the number of people who spoke English. Wyan took us from the city of Denpasar to adjoining villages that specialized in different crafts. One village deals exclusively in woodcarvings, another in gold and silver products, another in stonecarvings, one in weaving and yet another in art. Although the prices were higher than in 1980, things were still unbelievably cheap. I doubt that the men make any more than 5 cents an hour, if that much.

We visited the holy monkey forest, Tommy's favorite spot. Protected, well fed, and without any restraints, the monkeys had multiplied since 1980. They have seen so many tourists they had become quite brazen, and, I think, dangerous. On our first visit, we had hired a guide who carried a stick to protect us. Much to Doris's disgust, he had kept luring them onto her shoulder with peanuts. It made for great pictures, but I understood her revulsion. Tommy, on the other hand, was in his glory, with one monkey perched on his head and another on his hand. Lisa preferred to watch from a distance. We had to remind the kids not to clench their hands into fists, a sure way to get bitten, since the monkeys think you are holding peanuts. The second time we visited, we did not have a guide. One little monkey bit Lisa twice, but he did not break the skin. At that point, we wished we had hired a guide. So did the Danish couple who went in at the same time we did. One large monkey got on the women's head. She panicked and started to flail at the creature, which only infuriated him. We tried to get her to stand still, but she was hysterical. Finally the monkey had had enough, and, with several handfuls of hair, leaped to the ground. Needless to say, the Danish couple did not stay. We discovered that the best weapon was a rubber band. Workers in the rice paddies used slingshots to keep the monkeys out of the fields, and the sound of anything snapping usually scared them away.

We also went to fascinating dances and plays. The first was the Barong play, representing the struggle between good and evil. The Barong, a dragonlike creature, represents good; the Rangda, a monster with intestines hanging from its neck, represents evil. This story was about a mother of five who promised to sacrifice one of her sons to the evil monster. The lavish costumes were particularly intriguing. The expressions on the dragon were incredible, especially since the head is a wooden mask and the jaw moves. By using the jaw and their feet, the two men inside can convey any emotion. It was so realistic that Lisa was frightened and jumped into my lap. When we were there in 1980, Tommy had been only 3 years old, and he, too, had been frightened. He yelled "Appledore!" in the middle of the performance.

We also saw the Monkey Dance, featuring a 50-man chorus. The only music comes from the chorus, which sits and chants, "Kecak, kecak, cak" at different speeds and rhythms. They weave and chant for 20 minutes while a story is acted out within the circle they form with their bodies. The men use a lotion for their throats and are unable to talk for the next few days. The story concerns a divine prince forced to live with his wife and brother in exile, where an evil giant plans to steal the wife. The giant's prime minister disguises himself as a deer and lures away the man and his brother so the wife can be kidnapped. The husband, with the aid of a huge army of monkeys, kills the giant and rescues his wife.

Egg truck, Bali.

We bought our vegetables in the large, crowded market in Denpasar. After one walk through it, Tommy refused to go again. It was claustrophobic. It is located beneath a large concrete slab, above which are dingy clothing shops. Very little light filters in except around the edges, where hawkers sell slaughtered chickens that sit in the sun attracting flies from 5:00 a.m to 3:00 p.m. The aisles are so narrow that it is only possible to walk single file. You are literally hemmed in by rotting vegetables presided over by tired women. Somehow, children always manage to squeeze their way up to you. With big, almond eyes and dirty noses, they plead for a rupiah or two. Young girls also manage to make their way to you, quarreling about which one will carry your packages and how much it will cost you. "No, we don't need you" is not an acceptable answer. "No package, we'll carry the children." Lisa took it in stride, even though she made it known she didn't think much of the smelly place. Tommy, who was too big to be carried and too small to poke his head above the stands, was appalled. On our first trip, he had been the center of much attention. At that time, he had had sun-bleached snow-white hair, and the women could not keep their hands off him — almost as if touching his blond hair would bring them good fortune.

While I had the taxi driver, I purchased 26 dozen eggs and 30 loaves of bread. All the other items, such as fresh vegetables, we had brought back each day during our 10-day visit.

Crew member Ray Corbett left us in Bali, wanting to get back to the States. When Bob took him ashore to catch his plane, Lisa asked, "How is Ray getting back to the boat?" I told her he was not coming back, that he was flying home. This upset her. How could anyone fly home? What did that mean? I pointed out an airplane and told her he was going home on that and would be there the next day. She was confused. "How can anyone be home the next day when it has taken us forever to get here?" she asked.

The day of our departure brought the usual hassles of clearing port. First I had to go to immigration to be issued a sailing clearance; next it had to be stamped by customs; then it was on to the harbor police at the other end of town; back to the navy; and finally over to the office of the harbormaster, who had gone home for the day. I asked the taxi driver to take me to his home, where he invited me in. He explained that the stamp was at his office, so we went back into town and he opened the office. This would mean an overtime fee. Next I had to get the clearance signed by the port authority at his home.

The port authority officer signed my clearance for a small fee, and we were officially cleared. It had taken most of the day, and the permit was only good for 24 hours. If we did not depart, I would have to go through everything again and exchange more dollars for rupiahs.

By midafternoon, we started securing for sea. It was Bob's day to be on board. The rest of the crew was ashore and would not be back until the next morning. I was always thankful when they were all back on board, and it was not until we had actually departed that I breathed a sigh of relief.

Phosphate plant, Christmas Island.

Across the Indian Ocean

On the morning of August 31, we left Bali for Christmas Island, 580 miles away. The Indian Ocean is only relatively safe for a small boat crossing on the southerly route for about two months a year. In August and September, King Neptune whispers from the depths, "Come, children, cross me now." At other times, chances are about 70 percent that you will be caught in a cyclone. In August and September, it is only 5 percent. A serious cyclone is something no yacht can survive. We encounter gales and storms often, but a cyclone has winds of 150 m.p.h. Large ships avoid them by listening to the weather forecasts on short-wave radios, and they have the power and speed to get out of their paths. They can make 15 knots into a head sea. *Appledore* cannot sail into a head sea at all. We have to be content with 50 degrees off the wind, and if the sea builds up, it is more like 60 degrees. We could still change course if we received a report of a cyclone heading our way, but we did not have a short-wave radio on board. Our radio was VHF, with a range at best of 40 miles. This radio is widely used by all ships and shore stations, whereas a short-wave radio is very expensive. We had a good life raft, and we rationalized that it would not do us much good to be talking to someone on the radio 500 miles away if the boat was sinking out from under us. We also had an emergency position indicator (called an EPIRB), whose signals can be picked up by a ship, airplane, or satellite.

Our passage to Christmas Island began well. We had a fair breeze and a full moon, and what can be lovelier than a full moon reflecting across the sea or over a field of snow? It was remote, beautiful, and inspiring. It also felt good to be moving again, to see and hear the water rushing by the bow.

One morning, I made some popcorn for breakfast, much to the disgust of our crew. Of course, I did not force my taste on anyone, since breakfast was our meal of choice. Everyone prepared his or her own. Other options were Tang, oatmeal, toast, eggs, potatoes, beans, hash, coffee, and so forth. Another favorite of mine and Tommy and Lisa's was baked potatoes. These kept well and we always had a large supply on board. We were not so keen on eggs but kept them in stock for some of the boys who enjoyed them. We used about 10 dozen of them every 15 days.

On September 5, we arrived at Christmas Island and immediately filled our tanks with fresh water. We had not taken on fresh water in Bali because it was undrinkable. We only stayed here for two days, but a friendly yacht club welcomed us.

Christmas Island, belonging to Australia, is a major source of phosphate fertilizer for Australia and New Zealand. The phosphate is located near the surface in pockets and is intermingled with limestone rock formations. As the phosphate is removed by strip mining, the limestone is left, making it look like above-ground stalagmites. A reclamation program was in progress. There is no indigenous population, and the island's work force may drastically decrease when the phosphate mine is closed in a few years. The island was uninhabited until the mine opened and some 3,000 Malaysians were brought to the island to work.

On our first trip around the world, not many yachts had visited the island, and the Australians in charge had been extremely hospitable. We had even been invited to a cocktail party at the governor's house. One woman commented to Doris, "You yachties do as much good for us as we do for you. You make us get out of ourselves. We spend too much time being concerned with our own little group that we forget there are others in the world. Yachties bring a little excitement, something new to talk about, someone new to talk to." Five years later, in 1985, the number of visiting yachts per year had increased to more than 100, and the residents were not nearly as friendly. Yachties had begun to become a nuisance. The company store, which had gladly sold us goods in the past, had now doubled the prices for yachtsmen because of the high cost of resupplying their stocks.

We wondered what will become of the island if they close the mining operations as planned. Will the Malaysians stay or will this become a ghost island?

Our passage was fast to the next port of call, Direction Island in the Cocos-Keeling group. As we arrived on September 10, the winds were increasing steadily. Just before dusk, our foresail split a seam and we had to take it down for a quick sewing job. The Cocos Islands are also Australian and are used as a quarantine station to isolate animals before they are taken to Australia. Due to this keen concern about quarantining animals, we were asked to anchor outside of all the other yachts in case our hamster got out of his cage and decided to swim to freedom.

We stayed for two days and enjoyed Direction Island's beautiful beach. In the evening, just after dark, Doris and I took the kids ashore, where we used flashlights to search for hermit crabls. We saw hundreds of them running on the beach, each one carrying a shell on its back. Since Doris is an avid shell collector, the sight of all those shells scurrying about the beach was too much for her. Grabbing one large fellow, she got into a wrestling match with the crab inside for the rights to the shell. As she looked up, Tom and Lisa were staring at her. "Mom, what are you doing?" Tommy asked. "Oh, nothing," she responded, as she put the shell back down on the beach.

Direction Island had been a cable relay station 25 years earlier, but now all that was gone. The only telltale signs that it had ever existed were the cement foundations of the buildings that had been pushed over. The island had since been planted with coconuts. Of all the places we had stopped on our first world trip, this was the place Tommy remembered best. During the years that it took us to get back here, Tommy would often talk about the beach, the good times, and the coconuts we had picked.

While customs officials were clearing us, they asked if anyone needed a doctor. One of our crew had a mass of blisters under her arm that seemed to be spreading, so we had the doctor look at it. At first, he thought it was shingles, but he was not sure, so he gave her enough medication to cure any number of ills. After several other shipmates came down with it, including the kids, we checked with a doctor on Rodrigues Island. It turned out to be impetigo, something we felt sure we had caught from the laundry we had done in Bali.

While at Direction Island, we also met many friendly yachtsmen resting up for the big sail across the Indian Ocean. The Derek Blair family, with their two children and a 52-foot ferrocement boat, had come from New Zealand and were heading in the same direction as we were. Their boat was called *Hottyd*, an acronym for "Hold On Tight To Your Dreams." They hoisted anchor two hours before we did and we waved goodbye, but we should have said, "See you later," considering the way the next few weeks worked out.

On September 11 at 4:00 p.m., we set reefed sails and headed west. It was 2,000 miles to little Rodrigues Island, and there was no turning back. Once clear of the Cocos Islands, the wind and swell were back. This trip was a big challenge. I do not believe anyone can have a calm passage across this area of the ocean.

By dusk, we had caught up with and passed *Hottyd*, and all of us waved goodbye again. About 8:00 p.m., a squall came up with 35-knot winds, and we took down the mainsail, which already had a reef in it, and sailed with just the foresail and small staysail. The sea was running at

Doris watching a swell, Indian Ocean.

10 to 15 feet, and we were comfortable with this sail arrangement. Our speed was still good, so we settled down for the night. With just the foresail and staysail set, I knew we would need no further sailhandling.

In the morning, I called *Hottyd* on our VHF radio and he answered immediately. We compared positions from our latest satellite fixes, and he was now ahead of us by six miles. We looked but couldn't see him, since the sea was running high and the spindrift was flying. For two days, we stayed together but out of sight. First we would gain and pass him, then he would come on strong and catch up. The wind was steady, so we still had not put up our mainsail. One time when I was talking to Derek on the radio, an unfortunate thing happened. Their self-steerer had taken too great a strain and broke.

At noon, I called Derek again. We had not talked more than a minute when disaster struck again. The wind had gotten on the other side of their sail and they had jibed. The boom was badly bent, and their mainsail was out of commission for a while. The wind had increased and was gusting to 45 knots, with a large swell running. I didn't dare call Derek again, but he called us a few hours later and reported that his wife, Sookie, had just been caught off guard and thrown across the cabin, breaking her nose. His last words were, "Oh, well, the joys of yachting." This put a strain on everyone aboard *Hottyd*, but somehow Derek managed to keep everything together. Sookie was still able to steer, which was a help.

We were only three days from Cocos Island, but it was impossible to go back, and the wind and seas were increasing. Derek had a short-wave radio and reported that the weatherman was calling for a gale in our area, and a tropical depression was forming just north of our intended route. We put a reef in our foresail for the first time and watched some huge seas build. At 7:15 p.m., Tommy had come up on deck and we were watching the big waves to be sure to duck when spray came on board. It was getting dark when Tommy yelled, "Look at this one, Dad!" I turned and saw a monster, perhaps 30 to 40 feet. This would not usually be a problem, but this one was starting to break and curl over at the top. It was a sure sign of trouble.

I could see Tom diving down the hatch. Thank God he did that, I thought, because just then tons of water came on board, completely submerging me. The aft hatch was not closed and water went below, but fortunately it was a small hatch. At first I could just see the mast sticking up out of the water. Then the deck came up awash, like a submarine surfacing. Doris stuck her head up and asked if I was okay. "Just thoroughly soaked," I responded. I looked back at the next wave, but it was not nearly as high. It was getting dark, and we would not be able to see them coming for much longer. Luckily, these rogue waves do not come often.

When I was relieved at 8:00 p.m., I did not have to tell anyone to come on deck with a life harness. Everyone was wearing one. In the morning, the wind had dropped to 30 knots and we took out the reef. *Hottyd* was still within radio contact, although we never saw him again on this passage. At one time, we were 45 miles apart and the radio contact became weak, so we spent a few hours closing the distance. The two boats were well matched, and we stayed together just by trimming the sails slightly. The tropical depression just north of us remained there, and we were soon ahead of it. Our wind was steady and strong. The crew suggested we try to put one of them aboard *Hottyd* to help them steer. When Doris heard about the idea, she was adamantly against it. People got angry at her, but, as one of the owners of *Appledore*, she was as responsible as I was. She could just imagine what parents would say if we notified them that their child had drowned trying to swim from *Appledore* to another boat in the middle of the Indian Ocean.

In 13 days, we had Rodrigues Island in sight. As we made our way toward the small entrance in the reef to the harbor, a tremendous rain squall hit us. Full speed ahead on the engine just barely got us in. Since we were the only yacht — or, for that matter, the only vessel — visiting Rodrigues, we received royal treatment. We had free dockage and hundreds of people came down to see us, even old friends who remembered us from our last trip. I was especially happy to be back. We had just crossed a difficult part of the Indian Ocean, although we still had 2,000 miles to go to Durban. Some of the crew wanted to skip this island, as had been the case at Pitcairn. I told them that I was just stopping for them, that I had already seen it. They all ended up enjoying it, and, again, they were glad we had had the opportunity. Doris mentioned that she often felt that way when we came up on land after a long passage. You get into a routine and hate to break it unless there is something fantastic to see. The feeling is, "We are out here, let's just keep going." Her main objective was Durban, South Africa.

Hottyd decided not to stop at Rodrigues and continued on to Mauritius, where he hoped to order parts from England for his self-steerer.

In Rodrigues, we met Chrisnel Chooko, a happy man full of enthusiasm for life. Every morning, he came down to collect our laundry and would return it all washed and folded the next morning. One day, he noticed that Tommy's volleyball was flat, and he asked if he could fix it. In a few minutes, he was back with a smile on his face and the volleyball fully inflated. Since he had lost both legs well above the knees, he got around in a motorized wheelchair, a handmade three-wheeled job with a small gas engine. Someone always gave him a push to get it started, and often I saw a small child going for a ride with him. The whole population of Rodrigues seemed to be taking care of Chrisnel without making it very obvious. He wanted his picture taken with Lisa and Tommy, and I was glad to fulfill his wish. Apparently he was working on road construction when a truck ran over both legs. He was in a hospital for a month and gangrene set in. A United States naval destroyer came to the island and rushed him to the hospital in Mauritius, where his life was saved by the double amputation.

Another old friend, Paul Elysee, brought us two dozen eggs fresh from his chickens on the first day we arrived. He was in his seventy-second year and still going strong as the head longshoreman of the commercial dock. Just before we departed, he brought a present down to the dock for Tommy and Lisa, just as he had done the last time for Tommy. This time it was two sport jackets. Both Tommy and Lisa made good use of them, and I knew that Paul would feel satisfaction in that.

Rodrigues was one place where people felt and showed their thanks for all the aid the United States had sent. It was amusing to listen to them discuss American politics. In 1979, many had predicted that Edward Kennedy would win the next presidential election.

A man who had guided us to caves on the other side of the island also remembered *Appledore II*. A Brazilian boat had been there at the time, and our crews had rented a bus together. On the way back, there had been a great deal of partying. Our former guide laughingly remarked, "I'll never forget how many times the bus had to stop so you could pass water — not only the men, but the women, too."

The kids were a big hit, especially Lisa, who loved showing off to an appreciative audience. No matter what she did, someone would laugh. At times, she had the entire dockside laughing uproariously at her antics. She got angry one day, however, when she fell and they laughed, hurting her feelings. "I'm going to throw sand in their hair," she declared. Before she would go on deck again, I had to explain to her that they probably thought she was pretending. One afternoon, she almost disappeared when an 18-year-old girl wanted to take her home. Lisa was irate when we said no.

Rodrigues has a few unique hotels, and tourists can visit the island by making plane connections through Mauritius. The Point Venus Hotel sits high on a knoll, and the view of the Indian Ocean from the veranda is superb. Wicker chairs and rolled-up bamboo blinds lend it the atmosphere of a 1940s movie set. Unfenced goats graze around the grounds and cats curl up on vacant chairs. While sipping cold drinks, watching the sea below full of spindrift, we were thankful to be in port.

Conditions moderated on the morning of the fourth day, and we set sail once again. Each of us had spent a few hours sewing and inspecting the sails, which were beginning to show signs of wear. Our sails were made by Dave Bierig of North East, Pennsylvania, who had also made the sails for the other two *Appledores*. He is a great craftsman and did an excellent job cutting and stitching our 9-ounce main and jib and our 10-ounce foresail and staysail. The sail material was treated to protect against damage from ultraviolet light, but the thread had rubbed up against the lazyjacks and was wearing out, causing the seams to open up.

Our passage to Mauritius was fine, with a light following wind. The harbor of Port Louis is well lighted and therefore easy to enter at night, so we arrived uneventfully on September 30, just before midnight. The prime minister of Mauritius claims that Mauritius is a "secret island — once you have been there you always come back," and we were fulfilling his prophesy.

Mauritius exports sugar, without which the island would not survive, but 10 percent of it is used for making their famous Phoenix beer. The brewery can fill 28,000 small bottles per hour. Formerly a French overseas department, Mauritius now is independent and inhabited mostly by emigrants from India.

When I came up the companionway the morning after our arrival, a black man called for my attention and said he wanted to run errands for me. This is not an unusual request, but it can be difficult to find a good man. George had a different approach. He offered to let me hold his passport while he worked for me and also had a letter of reference from another yacht. His polite mannerisms impressed me. I had never used anyone for errands before, but since we had not cleared customs and could not go ashore, I asked him how much he wanted for getting us

Laundry woman,
Mauritius.

some fresh fruit and French bread. His price of $1.50 seemed fair enough, so I gave him $10 to get changed into rupees. He handed me his passport, but I said it was not necessary. I felt pretty good about him.

I was busy filling out the usual customs and immigration forms when George returned with fruit, bread, and my change. He told me that the bank was not giving the best exchange on the U.S. dollar, so he went to a money changer and got a better deal. I knew the rate because Rodrigues Island uses the same currency. When I paid him the $1.50, he asked if he could do anything else for us. We always have plenty of odd jobs to do in port, and since George was so inexpensive and enthusiastic, I asked him if he could fill our diesel jerry cans. I had a total of 10, holding about 60 gallons, and he said that would be no problem; the gas station was only two blocks away. He would do it for $3.00 and get a receipt. I handed him $150, and he tied the 10 cans together in two equal bundles, slung them over his shoulder, and was off.

After I cleared the boat with customs, I went over to visit another yacht that we had met on a previous passage. While there, another yachtsman who had been in Mauritius for a while came aboard, and I mentioned my good fortune — that I had someone getting my diesel fuel for me. He remarked, "I hope you didn't give him any money," and I told him I had. "Well, you can kiss that goodbye. You have just been taken." I told him that I did not think so. He said I was pretty naive and wanted to know if I wanted to place a bet on him. George had been gone for about an hour, and I declined the bet, but I said that I was quite certain George would return.

After lunch, when George had been gone for more than three hours, the fellow from the other boat came by and asked if I had seen my man yet. All I could say was, "Nope." "You're not going to," he told me. "One hundred and fifty dollars is a lot of money to people here. He can live on that for three months." He probably had a point, but this time it proved wrong. Just then, a pickup truck came rattling through the gate with George riding in the back on top of the full jerry cans. My doubtful friend looked at me and said, "That's your man, isn't it? Well, I'll be damned. You were lucky." So began our 10-day stay in Mauritius.

George did many more errands for us after giving me a reasonable explanation for what took him so long. He was not able to get the pickup truck until after lunch, so, in the meantime, he took some food home to his family. I gave him work even when we really did not need him, and he stuck to his price of $1.50 for an errand. He got everything for us — popcorn, flour, fruit, bananas, bread, even water. He always brought a receipt and the correct change. I also found him jobs on other yachts. When we left Mauritius, George was there to throw off our lines. "I'll be waiting for you," he said. I smiled, thinking, "Now there's a good reason to go around the world again."

In Mauritius, Andrea Avantaggio, 20, joined us. She was Kate's best friend and flew in from the United States. This brought us back up to a complement of five, which made for easier watches.

On our first voyage, we had received a letter from the commander of the tiny Mauritian navy, asking to be allowed to look at *Appledore II*. He had been thinking of getting a similar vessel to use for training. A dashing figure in his starched whites and spotless turban, he had warned us to leave Mauritius before the end of October because of the cyclone season. That year, the island was devastated by one of the worst cyclones in their history. We had not forgotten his warning, and we soon left for Réunion Island, en route to South Africa.

Réunion Island, a French department, was only 150 miles away, an overnight sail from Mauritius. We arrived on October 10 and sailed into the tiny harbor of Port-des-Galets. Very little English is spoken here, so at

*Tiny harbor of Port-
Des-Galets, Reunion.*

first it was difficult to get to know the place. Once we did, though, we found it interesting. Réunion, in fact, may be a better place for a vacation than Tahiti.

Although we had greatly enjoyed Bali and Mauritius, Réunion was like a breath of fresh air. It was clean, neat, and progressive, a welcome change. It was also much more expensive, however. We discovered French pastry and enjoyed the native cuisine; everything is stir-fried and served with rice.

We rented a car to visit the island's active volcano. Before arriving at the parking area and the walk to the crater, there is a vast expanse called the Plain of Sable, an area of loose brown rock that looks like velvet from a distance. However, if you attempt to drive on it as we did, your tires sink in and you get stuck. Doris, who had been urging me not to try it, asked sarcastically, "Now what?" "You and Tommy get out and push," I suggested. After several minutes of touch and go, I left them in a cloud of dust and regained the road. As she brushed herself off, Doris said, "Let's stick to the ocean, Herb! You're not too good on land."

The volcano erupted in 1983 but all that's visible now are the cone and the cooled, hardened rivers of lava. Doris said it looked like the chocolate cake she had baked when the boat had been rolling. We never did make it to the top of the crater, since it was a hike of several miles, but did walk to a small cone.

The next day, we drove to another mountain. Doris recalls:

My knuckles were white from gripping the car seat. It was not that I did not trust Herb's driving, although after the Plain of Sable, I had my doubts. In the States, these corkscrew roads would have been banned as unsafe. I liked their custom of putting a statue wherever someone had been killed in a car accident. However, the large numbers of them did not make me feel any more comfortable or relaxed. A religious cross at one turn was 5 feet high. I wondered if a bus or maybe a whole line of cars had gone over the cliff. It did not bother me going up nearly as much as coming down. Then I closed my eyes. I opened them once only to see a little old lady who apparently had some crippling disease like cerebral palsy making an awkward attempt to walk up the steep incline. By that point, I had little color left in my face, and we had 10 more miles to go before we got off that 25-mile snake. After watching a bus driver frantically turning the wheel to make a corner, I wondered what the life expectancy of a bus driver was here, and I began to wonder what mine was.

At the top of that murderous road had been a quaint little village with vineyards where they make the famous Ciloas wine, which fortifies people for the trip down the mountain, and the mineral baths where people have come for years to bathe and cure their arthritis. Over 7,000 people a year bathe in the tubs. It did not sound very sanitary to us, so we passed up the opportunity.

In usual Smith fashion, we managed to get beyond the end of the road in Ciloas and got hung up on a clump of sod. Herb was suggesting that I might have to push again, but I was thinking we were going to have to hire the townsmen to lift us off. Luckily, we were able to manage without either. The next day, when Herb suggested we spend the day at the beach, I was overjoyed.

On October 17, we departed for Durban on our last Indian Ocean passage, 1,500 miles. It is not a passage to look forward to, because the weather conditions can become extreme. We had to sail south of Madagascar, across the Mozambique Channel, and through the Agulhas current, which has a notorious reputation. One of the great ocean currents of the world, it runs mainly from northeast to southwest, following the 650-foot contour of the African continental shelf and diminishing over the Agulhas bank off the tip of South Africa. When southwesterly gales prevail against the southward-flowing current, exceptionally large waves build up. It is one of the very few places in the world where 70-to-100-foot waves have been encountered and large ships have been lost without a trace. Now there are warnings on the charts: "Abnormal waves may be encountered." The way to avoid the danger is to get out of the Agulhas current, but on this passage, we first had to cross it. I do not think that anyone else on board except Doris shared my apprehension. The more you know about the sea, the more respect you get for it.

In October 1870, Captain Wilhelm Schroder took the 499-ton German-built *Stephaniturm* on her maiden voyage from Europe to Madagascar. In Cape Town, Schroder, like the owners of the *Titanic* not many years later, boasted of her invincibility. One week later, he was one of only five people rescued after the ship capsized in raging seas near Durban. The wind at the time was only about 60 knots, not exceptional, but he said that he had "never seen such seas."

At first, we had some calm weather and made slow progress southward. The women, tired of the lack of success by the male membership, tried their luck at fishing. As luck would have it, something struck as soon as they put in the line. The line came off the reel with smoke, but since they didn't know how to stop it, a half-mile of line was gone before one of the men came to the rescue, grumbling about how long it would take to reel it in. But some time later they had on board a 20-pound mie mie, about the best-tasting fish there is.

On the fourth night out, we were rounding the southern end of Madagascar, about 75 miles offshore, when we were caught unexpectedly in a squall. *Appledore* had full sail up, but by running before the 50-knot wind, we managed to carry on without reducing canvas. The wind finally settled down to a northeast gale, and with the 2-knot Equatorial current setting us west, we made our best day's run — 234 miles in 24 hours. The next evening, four hundred miles from Durban, the wind became calm and we started motoring, pulling away from the bad weather. Behind us, we could see lightning hitting the water; ahead, the sky was full of stars.

During the next day, we continued to make about 5 knots under power. I had enough fuel to motor all the way to Durban if necessary. Although the sea was like glass, a rather large swell coming from the south reminded us that we were trying to sneak across a sleeping giant. At any moment, we could be hit by a southwest front. That's part of the challenge of sailing around the world, reaching a new goal, Durban; It lifts your life above the ordinary. On our last voyage, we had been hit by a southwest front just before Durban, and while visiting Durban, a southwester came through about every three days. I knew what to expect.

Just 60 miles from Durban, in the middle of the Agulhas current, a thick cloud bank developed in front of us. It did not look good, but there was no wind in it — just a little drizzle. The clouds would have made it difficult if using a sextant to find our position by the stars, but the Sat-Nav was working perfectly. When we were 40 miles from Durban, I called harbor control on the radio and they reported calm winds. In eight hours, a lot can change, but this time our luck held. Thus, on October 27 at 3:00 a.m., we sailed into Durban Harbor. This was a significant event for Doris and me. We would be able to take it easy for a month and enjoy the countryside with the boat safely tied up.

Sailing off Cape Town.

Zebra, Kruger National Park.

South Africa

South Africa is one country we truly had enjoyed five years before, and this time we were looking forward to visiting Kruger National Park. Since we were one of the first visiting international yachts of the season, we had the whole international pier practically to ourselves. It was in front of the Point Yacht Club, well protected from exposure to wind and sea.

Four days later, we doubled up the lines, rented a car, and drove inland. Unlike many boats that arrived in Durban, we now had an experienced crew that I felt good about. Although most yachtsmen just lock up their boats and go ashore, someone would be on board ours at all times. Since we all shared the in-port duty days by doubling up in Durban, we would have two days on and 10 days off.

It is about 400 miles to Kruger National Park from Durban, and we drove there in one day. Kruger is the same size as Massachusetts and has more different species of animals (122) than any other game reserve in the world. The park is named for South African President Paul Kruger, who first proposed it in 1898. In Kruger are approximately 8,600 elephants, 29,000 water buffaloes, 95,000 impalas, 26,000 zebras, 15,500 blue wildebeest, 5,000 giraffes, 7,400 kudu, 2,300 hippos, 750 black rhinos, 1,500 lions, 700 leopards, and 300 cheetahs— just to name some of the more abundant species.

Driving along the many roads that cross the park, we saw most of the above-mentioned animals. At night, we entered a fenced-in compound and stayed in a deluxe hut with toilet, shower, and air-conditioning. Since it was the off season, we could stay at a different camp each evening. In December, January, and February, the park is full and reservations are needed well in advance. It cost just $32 (South African) for a family of four to stay overnight; the evening meal in the restaurant was $21. We were getting $2.70 (South African) for every United States

183

dollar, which helped make it an inexpensive vacation. It was a majestic sight to watch the sun set over the grasslands and through the branches of the baobab trees, with a herd of elephants or water buffaloes roaming free down to a stream. It was a much better experience than I had ever imagined, and the two children loved it. What makes it so interesting is that you have to go out and find the animals yourself. Dawn or dusk is the best time for seeing the most animals.

One evening we hit the jackpot and saw 16 different species; once, at 4:30 a.m., we saw nothing. We took more than 400 slides to document our visit, and it was the first time Doris ever showed an interest in using a camera. It had its advantages. One afternoon, we came upon an elephant at the edge of the road. I wanted a closeup, so I moved in with the car as near as I dared. "Herb, I don't want a picture of the hairs on his chin. You see that tree he's toppling? That could be us!" The elephant was doing an admirable job of uprooting a tree to feed on the roots. I didn't get any closer. From the way Doris's hands were shaking, I was afraid she wouldn't get any worthwhile pictures.

The kids' favorite animal was the warthog. Its skinny tail stands up as straight as a pole, and a little globe of hair bounces merrily at its tip. One fellow, very upset with us, stopped dead in his tracks and looked at us challengingly: "Come out and fight like a man." Sensing victory, he gave us a contemptuous look and jauntily continued on his way. The car was filled with the children's laughter.

On the morning that I announced we would be heading back to Durban, everyone moaned. Our duty day was coming up soon.

Durban is one of the cleanest, safest cities we have ever visited, and it offers great stores, great theaters, a beautiful white sandy beach, and all the touristy shops and amusements to go with it.

At the dock, a Norwegian boat rafted up to us. Aboard was a little girl named Tina who was a year older than Tommy. She had gone to school in California and spoke English like an American. The minute she spied Tom, she was determined to be with him every single moment. The first morning, she came over at 5:00, but after I explained that he didn't get up until at least 8:00, she went back to her boat and I got back in bed. We took them to Expo and her father took them to the dolphin show. For one week, until Tina's family left for Cape Town, the two were inseparable.

One day, I found them sitting side by side in the main cabin reading a Willard Price book. Her parents had already noticed a major change in her personality. Their sullen, unhappy little girl had become a happy, energetic member of their crew again. We noticed a similar change in Tom. It must have been difficult not having playmates. Adult companionship is not the same.

By the end of three weeks, so many foreign yachts had arrived that five of them were rafted up beside us, meaning heavy traffic across our deck. Finally, we were asked to anchor out, to give other boats a chance to tie up. We had to anchor about a quarter-mile out, setting out all four of our anchors — two off the bow and two off the stern. We wanted to be prepared for the southwesters that we have seen come through at 70 knots. It was not as inconvenient as we expected. We rented the taxi launch from Bay Services and called on the radio when we wanted to go ashore. They operated night and day.

The Durban Yacht Club is one of the best in the world for cruising yachts. Not only did we get to use the showers and bar, but they served inexpensive meals. On Sundays, they also had a movie. They don't celebrate Thanksgiving Day, but they had a special turkey dinner for the visiting yachts.

On December 2, we were ready to depart for Cape Town. I had done the necessary legwork and checked out with immigration, harbor revenue, customs, and the port captain. The only thing left was to call the harbor control office. Before I did that, however, I checked with the weather office at the airport one more time. A forecaster there said he could see that a low-pressure area was developing 300 miles south of Durban. It did not look good, so I decided to delay the departure for 12 hours to see what was going to happen.

In 12 hours, it had become a coastal storm, with strong winds forecast. A gale would be okay for *Appledore* if the wind was going to be from a favorable direction to push us down the coast, but the wind that was forecast was from the southwest, which would have been dead against us. So we waited for the storm to move north.

When it hit Durban two days later, the wind reached 50 knots, accompanied by some spectacular lightning that looked as though it hit every high-rise building in Durban. The next day, it was sunny and perfect, although another coastal low was coming. Again we delayed our departure, and, after a week, we were still waiting to leave. I was becoming concerned that we would not get to Cape Town for Christmas. By the third attempt, customs and immigration officials were getting to know me quite well, and the paperwork was becoming easier. It looked good. No bad weather was predicted for 24 hours. We departed on December 11, but two miles outside the breakwater, the saltwater cooling pump on the engine quit, overheating the engine. I took it apart at least 10 times and completely rebuilt it, but still I could not get it to work properly, so we returned to Durban, towing *Appledore* with our outboard-powered skiff.

We anchored at 11:00 p.m. Customs came down to clear us back in, even though we had not gone anyplace. Just about then, I tried to use the engine to set the anchors when the cooling pump suddenly started working. Something had clogged the discharge line, which I had overlooked. The volume of water was greater than we had seen for six months, so we hoisted the anchors back on board and departed. It was midnight and we were soon sailing south on a favorable wind, making excellent speed in the Agulhas current.

In 24 hours, we were 160 miles down the coast, but the barometer was dropping. From the weather patterns of the previous six weeks, I figured we had about 24 hours before a southwest front hit us. I decided to go into East London, a port we had visited on our previous voyage. Just as we sailed into the harbor, the southwest wind began to stir. Two hours later, gale warnings were broadcast, and we remained tied up in East London for two days.

It was now December 15, and we still had 500 miles of coastal sailing before us to reach Cape Town for Christmas. We were all getting anxious. I felt strongly that it would be great to get around the Cape of Good Hope and be back in the Atlantic by the New Year. We were able to depart from East London on December 15, bound for Cape Town direct. We had a fair but light breeze.

In a couple of days, within 75 miles of Cape Agulhas, another gale warning was broadcast on Cape St. Blaize radio, just as we were getting out of the station's range. There would be no other stations within range until we reached Cape Town. Fortunately, we were just passing Mussel Bay, which has a manmade harbor protected by two breakwaters, so we entered at 1:00 a.m. A good-sized swell foamed against the breakwaters on both sides, and we tied up alongside a fishing pier.

In the morning, we heard an old-fashioned sound coming from the freight yard — a steam whistle. Everyone stuck their heads up the hatch and there, to our amazement, was a steam locomotive shuffling cars around the yard. On our last voyage to South Africa, we had seen many steam engines, but now they were getting scarce. It was a real treat to be able to show Tommy and Lisa a working one. It was hauling passengers to the next town, Hartenbos, 10 miles away, and we later bought tickets. William Strick, the engineer, gave us a ride in the engine cab. He was a young man and a fourth-generation steam engineer. His great- grandfather had come from Ireland. We were showing such a keen interest in the engine that he gave us the grand tour. Engine number 3684, class 24, was about 42 years old. Mr. Strick gave Tommy one of the wornout brass handles used for turning on the steam. To heat their coffee, they attach the pot to a metal rod and slide it into the firebox. It doesn't take long.

That evening at 9:00, the wind began to increase; within an hour, it was blowing 50 knots. A swell started coming into the harbor and

Steam engine, Mussel Bay.

pounding us up against the dock. It was the same situation that we had in Punta Arenas when we cracked our railcap. Before this could happen again, we got away from the dock and moved to a more protected part of the harbor. A few other yachts did likewise, and one came over to tie up next to us. As he was approaching, however, he lost control of his vessel and started to ram us. I managed to fend him off, so the blow didn't cause any damage to *Appledore*, but my finger got caught in the lifeline and was broken — a stupid mistake on my part.

At 11:30 p.m., I wandered around the streets of Mussel Bay looking for a hospital and came upon Constable Fletcher, who told me the hospital was five miles away and offered me a lift. When he dropped me off, he expressed sincere sympathy and said he would wait for me. I told him he should not bother because I was going to be there for a while, and he said, "I'll be back for you then, after I make some rounds."

Two hours later, he was waiting outside the front door when I came out. He asked how the finger was and I told him, "Compound fracture. They want me back at 8:00 a.m." Again I was quite moved by his compassion. This police officer had a heart. I thought of all the hard times South Africa was having and hoped Constable Fletcher would not be involved. He brought me back to *Appledore* at 2:00 a.m., wished me a Merry Christmas, and said he hoped the finger would be feeling better soon. He asked if we would be staying for Christmas, and I said there was a good possibility of it, but as I stepped out of his warm truck, I could feel that the wind had moderated. I knew we would be getting underway at dawn. "Take care of yourself," I told him, and I closed the door. As he drove off, I thought about something my father had told me a long time ago: "The true measure of a man is his heart, not the color of his skin." Constable Fletcher was black and a black police officer in South Africa has a different and difficult life.

At 5:00 a.m., I sat on deck alone, watching the sunrise; everyone else was asleep. The red morning sky was impressive. The sun soon emerged as a brilliant dark red ball out of a gray sea, and I thought, "Red in the morning, sailors take warning; red at night, sailors delight." But we had to depart or we would have no chance to make Cape Town for Christmas. I woke everyone and we left.

It was just 190 miles to Cape Town, and I figured we could make that in a couple of days, arriving three days before Christmas. We would have to sail around Cape Agulhas, Danger Point, and the Cape of Good Hope, but the weather experts were calling for light winds — for perhaps six hours.

At first, there was no wind, and a tremendous black thunderstorm moved off the land out to sea, just missing us. We used the engine to motor south at 5 knots. At dusk, a 25-knot northwest wind was blowing, and we began tacking. During the night, with only half of our sails up, we made only 12 miles to the south. It was now December 20. Since we were about 30 miles offshore, I decided to try for smoother conditions and a more favorable current closer to the shore. We hoisted full sail and spent all morning on an inshore tack.

By noon, we were only a mile from shore. We could plainly see the desolate coast and the lighthouse at Cape Infanta. Just about then, the wind started backing to the southwest, the worst possible direction for us. Now we had to tack right into the wind and the building seas. Each hour, the waves grew bigger, yet we made 40 miles by dark. *Appledore* was giving us an exciting ride, driving through and over the cresting waves harder than ever before with full sail set. Cape Agulhas Light was visible only eight miles away, and, once past the light, we would be able to fall off and have the wind on our beam. One more tack into 20-foot seas saw us clear of Cape Agulhas, the southernmost tip of Africa (not the Cape of Good Hope, as many believe). We were now on the home stretch, with 90 miles to go and making 8 knots with a fair breeze. Morale was high. It was December 21 and we would be in Cape Town for Christmas — or so we all believed.

At 11:00 a.m., we passed the Cape of Good Hope, site of the world's most powerful lighthouse, and then we were back in the Atlantic Ocean. Hundreds of seals approached the boat and played in our wake. The water temperature was a chilly 52° on the Southern Hemisphere's longest day of the year. It felt cool. Our ship-to-shore radio had been on all night, and, just after passing the Cape of Good Hope, we heard an urgent broadcast. "All ships, all ships. This is Cape Town Radio calling all ships. Received at Cape Town at 0900 GMT — gale warnings. I repeat, gale warnings from Orange River to the Cape of Good Hope."

I thought we might just get in before it hit, but the wind had been increasing for an hour, and things change as fast in this region as they do on the southern coast of Argentina. We had only 22 miles to go and were passing the Twelve Apostles, a dozen majestic peaks running along the coast, when a local boat called and reported the wind at 60 knots off Lion's Head, only 10 miles ahead of us. We started lowering sails — first the main, then the staysail. By then, the wind was up to 40 knots. Next we took down all sails, and blasts of wind coming off the mountains reminded me of the williwaws in the Strait of Magellan. At the moment, it was a beam wind, but once around Green Point, it would be a headwind, and we would have to tack against it into Cape Town Harbor.

I was not sure we could do it, but we put up the reefed foresail to give it a try. Fortunately, the wind was coming off the land, and since we were close to shore, not much of a sea was building. Harbor control reported the wind at the harbor entrance to be 55 knots, and, after a few tacks, we made no progress. Therefore, as we came through the next tack, all hands popped the reef out and quickly hoisted full foresail like a fully trained racing crew. We had some power now and went through the tacks faster.

I could see Doris pacing nervously, as she often does when she is worried about the boat. She kept eyeing the rigging as the sails luffed violently through each tack. Luckily, our sails had just been restitched, and even though they took a beating in these conditions, they held. We approached the outer breakwater of Cape Town Harbor and soon were past it. A few more tacks brought us into the inner harbor, with very little room to maneuver. The men in harbor control, we were told later, had been watching us closely with their binoculars. The little wooden gaff-rigged schooner from Maine was showing her true colors tacking against a 55-knot southeast gale going to windward. *Appledore* is traditionally rigged like all Maine windjammers — old-fashioned perhaps, but time-proven and reliable.

After a few more tacks, we approached the main shipping dock, and Chris stood ready to jump off with the bow line. We rounded up into the wind and dropped the sail. Full speed ahead on the engine held us alongside the dock as we got the bow line secured. Having finally arrived in Cape Town, just three days before Christmas, we were all in a joyous mood. I had my finger taken care of by a hand specialist. It was a mess.

Gale-force winds continued for two days, but Christmas Day was like a typical Maine summer day, with fog burning off early. It was a beautiful Christmas, and, yes, Santa Claus does visit South Africa.

Outside the post office, Mussel Bay.

Cape Town is a great city. It has friendly people, modern hospitals (including the one that performed the first heart transplant), excellent theaters, spectacular views of the city from Table Mountain and Lion's Head, and impressive Christmas lights. After spending almost a year in less-developed countries, South Africa was a real treat.

In Cape Town, we were made honorary members (for a small fee) of the Royal Cape Yacht Club, where we could take showers, have snacks and cold drinks (the outside temperature was 80°), or just sit in a real chair and relax. The club also had a slipway, so we hauled out *Appledore* and spent a couple of days scraping and painting her bottom for the third time. We hired a local man to help sand the topsides but soon came to regret it, because he left many a dip in our previously smooth hull. Doris had always been protective of the hull, preferring to paint it herself rather than to have to spend the next week sanding off runs. After she saw what the man had done with the sander, she was more determined than ever to do it herself. The rest of the people on board were a little upset that she would not let them paint, but they didn't understand the feelings of protectiveness associated with building your own boat.

By the time we reached South Africa, we had gotten the missing wind generator parts and put it to use. With the winds in Durban and in Cape Town, we were able to keep our refrigerator and the lights running without having to use our engine very much. My only fear was that the

Tom going ashore, Cape Town.

generator would fall apart in the strong wind gusts and one of its blades would decapitate someone. In one particularly bad blow, Doris and I wrestled the thing down, a procedure so dangerous that I vowed never to use it again. I sold it in the Virgin Islands.

Table Mountain makes an impressive backdrop for the city. To get to the top, you can take a cable car. On our first trip up, the wind howled at the 3,600-foot summit. Soon after we arrived, the officials were asking everyone to return to the base, because even higher winds were expected. Table Mountain has always been used as the local weather forecaster. When white clouds racing up from the Cape of Good Hope spill over the top and cascade down the side, it looks as though a tablecloth has been placed over it. This is a sure signal that a gale can be expected within 12 hours. The sign never failed to be correct while we were there. We had a gale about every three days, and the wind often reached 70 m.p.h. in the city.

We met a couple of fisherman from a Polish factory ship tied to another pier. They wanted to practice their English and invited us to take a look at their ship. Their staterooms were immaculate and were inspected every morning as if they were in the military. They gave us glasses of vodka and grapefruit juice and showed us pictures of their homeland. Doris noticed that they had a pinup calendar on the wall. "Is that a picture from home too?" she teased. "Oh, no, Polish women would never do that!" They spend months at sea away from their families. I felt lucky to have mine with me.

The waters off the Cape of Good Hope mark the divide between the

Atlantic and Indian oceans. We drove the 40 miles from Cape Town to the Cape of Good Hope and spent an enjoyable day visiting a national park that has an abundance of wildflowers and baboons. We made many other excursions around the countryside without any problems, and none of our crew members experienced any difficulty. We were told by one cab driver that there would be trouble on Christmas Day but that we would not see it. In fact, we never heard that it materialized. We did stay away from the black townships, where there were rumors of trouble. When we were in Durban, we had heard that tension was higher in Cape Town, but we did not notice anything different.

In her log, Doris wrote:

> All over the Cape Town area, the baboons run wild. It is illegal to feed them because that makes them very dangerous to humans. I had gotten out of the truck we had borrowed to take a picture when one large male came over and grabbed my dress. I screamed and Tom and Herb started running toward me to scare him away. From that time on, I refused to get out of the truck or even to roll down my window. My fears were permanently galvanized that same afternoon when I watched a baboon pull the wig off a woman who had been feeding him from a car window. Apparently the woman had run out of food, and the baboon was jumping about nervously. Suddenly he put his arm through the window and grabbed what looked like hair. I thought he scalped her, and I didn't dare look for fear of what I would see. The next moment, I heard the door open and saw the woman tear off into the bush after him. When she came out of the bush, she had her wig in her hands. The baboon followed her back to the car and sat beneath her window, looking contrite. Then he began his slow, vigilant begging again.

We had rediscovered the cinema in Durban and Cape Town, where the theaters were large and plush. It was a pleasure just to be able to sit in one. We saw more than 14 movies, many of them twice. The Camel cigarette commercials, depicting America and its way of life, made us homesick. I wondered what people thought about the United States after they watched Charles Bronson in *Death Wish III*.

Travelers on train, Mussel Bay.

Chris painting the hull, Cape Town.

Chris and Andrea reading mail.

South Atlantic Islands

On January 25, we departed Cape Town with a new crew member, Liz Corbett, 20, who replaced her father, Ray. She fit in beautifully. There is often a worry when picking up a new crew member in the middle of a voyage. Fortunately, Andrea and Liz both were accepted the minute they came on board.

Just outside the harbor, we sighted five humpback whales, and had a slight northwest headwind. With the wind came thick fog, but it did not last long, and by dusk, the wind had gone around to the southeast. We were off.

The trip across the South Atlantic Ocean represented to most of us the beginning of our homeward passage. It was 1,700 miles to Saint Helena, and a fresh southeast wind took us all the way. We never had to use the engine, which was especially welcome because we would need the diesel for getting through the doldrums at the equator. Tommy, who continuously trailed a fishing line behind the boat, was interrupted from school lessons a couple of times to haul in a fish.

After 13 days of good sailing, we arrived at Saint Helena, site of Napoleon's exile after his capture by the British at Waterloo. Rudyard Kipling reflected the British point of view:

> How far is St. Helena from the fields of Waterloo?
> A near way, a clear way the ship will take you soon
> A pleasant place for gentlemen with little left to do!

According to a historical researcher, a member of Napoleon's entourage had a less flattering view. "The devil must have shit the island as he flew from one world to another." Napoleon is said to have hated the confines of Saint Helena and its disagreeable climate, and he certainly disliked being kept under surveillance by his captors. Until his death in

195

Napoleon's house, St. Helena.

1821, he lived a lonely, unhappy life in a house now restored as a museum. Although the island belongs to Britain, the small acreage upon which his house stands is owned by France. A few years after his death, the French came to collect his remains and take them to France.

Although the coast is dry and its plant life is dominated by cactus, the higher elevations here are green, lush, and cool. Jamestown, the main community, is located in a narrow ravine, an odd place to build a town, but it was close to a natural bay where ships could unload supplies. In the old days, when it rained, the ravine became a river, but they built a dam at its head a few years ago. Today the town is thriving, with a dozen stores and a hotel. A ship calls every two months. There is no airport on Saint Helena, so it's a two-month visit or none at all.

Our only problem was getting ashore. We were fortunate on this trip that the surge was not too bad, but getting out of the skiff is tricky. At the crest of the swell, you have to lunge for a line hanging from a post and then swing yourself ashore. A miss guarantees a dunking.

The people here have a warmth and generosity toward strangers not found very often on many other islands. Maurice Thomas, for example, saw us hiking along the road toward Napoleon's house, a journey of about five miles, and stopped to give us a lift. At Longwood, where the house is located, a friendly man named Mr. Crowie ran the small general store, and George Benjamin and his wife gave us a ride back to Jamestown. George has been the museum guide for many years.

In port at the same time was an 11-foot 10-inch boat called *Acrohc Australic*, which would become the smallest boat ever to sail around the world. Sergio Testa, 40, had sailed alone from Australia in his little boat. One evening, we invited him over for supper. He told us that he fell asleep accidentally one night when he was sailing around South Africa. When he woke up at dawn, all he saw was sand. During the night, he had sailed up on a beach. Local fishermen helped him get his boat back in the water and he continued his voyage. Sergio built the boat himself out of aluminum. At Saint Helena, he was waiting for a supply ship that was bringing money from his brother. He was flat broke.

We stayed three days at Saint Helena and left on February 10. It was an easy downwind sail to Ascension Island, 700 miles away. The wind was light at times, however, and on some days we only made 75 miles. Ascension Island is owned by England, but there is no British government support or local government. England leased the island to private companies, which hired administrative personnel to keep things running smoothly. The four major tenants are the United States Air Force, Pan American Airlines, British Broadcasting Corporation, and the Cable and Wireless Company. There are hundreds of strange antennas and satellite dishes on the island Yachts are allowed to stay only 48 hours, and we had to be back on board at 6:00 p.m. unless we had a sponsor. I had to provide medical insurance for each person on board before they could go ashore. It was available on the spot for $45.

During the Falklands War, the airport at Ascension Island was allegedly the busiest in the world for two days. But other than that one claim to fame, the island is dull and has a very inhospitable, hot terrain. Dry volcanic rocks, including many large fragments, cover the island. One piece took on the perfect form of a dinosaur, and the surface in many areas looks more like that of the moon than of the earth.

On Ascension Island is a spot called Comfortless Cove, used in the mid-1800s as a dropoff for yellow-fever victims. Ships from Africa often had passengers who contracted the dreaded disease, and the sick were left in the cove in order to save their crews. Islanders would leave food for them among the moonlike rocks. If the person recovered, he would walk out; if not, he would be buried in the small cemetery surrounded by spears of volcanic rock. On the gravestones, we found the names of people from at least four different ships, all dating back to the 1830s. It was an eerie, silent place. Doris said it was so oppressive that her ears would not stop popping. Not that we had to worry, but we had had yellow-fever vaccinations before we left the United States.

The one redeeming spot on the island is a vegetable farm located on 10 acres of grass atop the highest mountain. The peak is just high enough to pierce the tradewind clouds and collect rain. All other fresh water comes from a diesel desalinating plant; water on Ascension is more costly than electricity.

On our arrival, I had the good fortune to meet Ed Scipio, a dockworker who had come to Ascension from Saint Helena on an 18-month contract. He sponsored us all so we could remain ashore until 11:00 p.m. This was very generous, since he did not know us and had to accept responsibility for our good conduct. We were especially grateful to have a sponsor because an extraordinary event occurs at night on Ascension Island.

Each year, giant sea turtles come across the 1,200 miles of open ocean from Brazil to lay their eggs on the beaches here. At night, they come ashore and crawl up on the beaches to dry sand and start digging with their flippers. We were able to watch them under a full moon. They appeared in the breakers on the wet sand, took 10 minutes to look around, and then started moving laboriously up the beach. While we were lying in the sand watching them, I felt something crawling up my leg. Reaching down, I found a newly hatched turtle not more than 3 inches long. We examined it with our flashlights and then let it go. It was amazing how it continued its relentless journey down to the sea.

Some of the turtles coming out of the surf had shells that were 5 feet from end to end and weighed hundreds of pounds. Lisa and Tommy were particularly excited by all this. When a turtle started digging, sand flew in every direction for 20 feet, and a crater began to appear. In 30 minutes, it was down 2 feet. Then it crawled out and started another hole. Apparently they dig several of these holes to confuse predators. Finally, at the last hole, about two hours after coming ashore, it very carefully digs a small hole with its back flippers and drops in 30 or 40 eggs. We stayed downwind and observed them from a very close range. They never knew we were there. After covering the holes, they started back down to the sea, exhausted, and we returned to the boat with yet another memory.

We departed from Ascension Island at 2:00 a.m., having stayed only 20 of our allotted 48 hours. If we had stayed longer, I would have had to pay additional medical insurance fees. Such extra charges need to be taken into account by anyone planning a round-the-world cruise. On our first circumnavigation, there were few extra fees. Now almost every port has them. In South Africa, it cost a dollar a day for each crew member at the Royal Cape Yacht Club. In Australia, they wanted a departure tax of $20 per person. And there are always port fees for the boat. It is best to take along a lot of cash. We received our worst bill on our first world trip when we entered French Guiana. The officials were not convinced that I had a pleasure yacht, and they charged us $750 for pilot's fees, a service we had not used, and agent's fees for a man named Ho You Fat, whom we did not want as an agent. "Americans are not kings here," they were quick to point out. Despite my complaints, I could not escape paying the bill.

Tom and the Pitons, St. Lucia.

To the Caribbean

It is 3,000 miles from Ascension Island to Barbados, the longest passage of this voyage. We started out with a following breeze but in five days, as we approached the equator, we were becalmed and hot. The sea was a sheet of glass and we were in the doldrums. For the next six days, we had to use the engine, but at least we were prepared for this with two extra 55-gallon drums of diesel fuel lashed on deck. In the old days, one ship without auxiliary power reportedly spent 86 days becalmed here. The high-pressure system of the Northern Hemisphere converges here with the high-pressure system of the Southern Hemisphere and there are many squalls with thunder and lightning. It's almost like walking under a coconut tree. You just hope that one doesn't hit you.

At one point, I counted five different squalls drifting slowly east to west. Many times, we could avoid them simply by changing course a few degrees. I thought of Captain Nabb, on the USCG icebreaker *Eastwind*, who used to change course whenever possible to go around a squall. If he thought that was wise with a steel icebreaker, surely it would also be a good idea for a wooden Maine windjammer. It was not popular with the people armed with bottles of shampoo and bars of soap, but they did not object when one cell we were avoiding let loose a burst of lightning only yards away.

After we crossed the equator and initiated our three new crew members — Bob, Andrea, and Liz — into the shellback fraternity, the wind picked up from the northeast. Ordinarily, the northeast trades wouldn't appear as close to the equator, but they were filling in nicely. We shut off the engine, trimmed the sails, and set a direct course of 320° magnetic for Barbados, then about 1,600 miles away. The northeast trades took us all the way, and we had some good days of sailing, averaging 150 miles a day at about 6 knots.

During this passage, when I was steering at 4:30 one morning, a shooting star streaked across the sky, illuminating the sails with a white light as if someone had shone a spotlight on them. The meteorite then broke into three pieces, with orange flames trailing behind each. We had seen shooting stars every night, but nothing like this. The fireballs broke up like a Fourth of July display. I wondered how many actually hit the earth. At sea, we see thousands of stars on a clear night, and it is still mind-boggling to try to comprehend our universe or even our galaxy. Just how many more worlds are out there?

At noon on March 5, we crossed our outward bound track at 4° north latitude and 41° west longitude. We had sailed around the world.

It is difficult to imagine how much you will miss something until you are forced to go without it. On board *Appledore*, we did not have flush toilets, showers, air-conditioning, television, electric stove, refrigerator, running water, or much space. Therefore, after our 50-day passage from South Africa to Barbados, with only brief stops at Saint Helena and Ascension, we were ready to indulge in a few of these modern conveniences. Two hours after we arrived, we all sat down for cheeseburgers and french fries at Knowles Dockyard Restaurant. It was only a simple meal with a cold glass of milk, something we all have had most of our lives, but what pleasure it gave us this time! Perhaps that is our best argument for making a voyage around the world. We don't take as much for granted anymore. I find I can appreciate the United States a lot more — partly because of our so-called modern conveniences, but even more because of our freedoms.

Shortly after we crossed the equator, we picked up a strong breeze, and the boat began to pitch and roll. Doris had a bad case of seasickness — or so we thought. One day she asked me if I still wanted 10 kids. I was delighted. Not feeling well, she did not share my enthusiasm. In Barbados, a doctor confirmed that she was pregnant; Susan Margaret would be born in October.

Barbados is a low, warm, friendly island with a few passenger ships arriving daily. From our anchorage, we could see Halley's Comet and the Southern Cross. We spent a week there and everyone was in the partying spirit, although it wasn't necessary to leave the boat to hear the music. The crew's favorite disco was located on the beach, a few yards from where we were anchored, and it blared music until the wee hours of the morning. I wondered how people could actually be in there and not go deaf. The one problem with the partying was the need to pick up everyone by skiff. One evening — or rather morning — at 4:00, one of the boys swam back to the boat. I shook my head in disbelief but said little, since he felt bad enough. His shoe had fallen overboard and was floating away, and he had to jump back in to retrieve it.

Susan at the helm.

A short overnight sail away was Martinique which is as French as Paris. Small sidewalk cafes dot the city, wine and cheese fill half of the grocery stores, and everything is expensive. A dozen eggs cost $3 (U.S).

In Fort-de-France, where we anchored, we met an unusual man, Heinz Stucke, 41, from West Germany. He had been riding a bicycle around the world for 23 years. His goal was to visit every country in the world, and he had already been to 153. The bicycle had been welded up many times, and his yearly budget was limited. "However," he told us, "this is the way I meet people. I need them. If I was wealthy, perhaps I would not put up with the hassles of dealing with the locals. Instead, I would have supplies flown into checkpoints and live in hotels." Heinz showed us a world map with his track and the dates marked on it. There are few places he hasn't visited. He flies over the oceans but starts pedaling just outside the airports. I noticed a large scar across his

*John
Sowden
and
Tarmin.*

forehead and asked what had happened. He had been run down by a
truck in South America. I asked him if he had ever been attacked. He said
no. Heinz had many tales to tell, and I wondered why I had never read
about this amazing man. He had already been to the United States and
Canada and he hoped to visit China soon after we saw him. He had
visited Russia but was not allowed to ride his bike across the country. He
had had a color brochure printed with 25 pictures showing his travels. On
his tour through Spain, he had just sold 10,000 of them for $1 each.

Another unusual man whom we saw in Martinique was John
Sowden, a 66-year-old bachelor. We were old friends, having met in St.
Lucia on our last voyage and again in Durban on this voyage. John has to
be the greatest singlehanded sailor in this century, but few know about
him because he is not a publicity-seeker. He had just completed his third
solo circumnavigation in his tired 25-foot wooden sloop *Tarmin*, a record
accomplishment. No other man has done this three times alone and under
sail, and I doubt that any ever will with the same wooden boat. Tom
Blackwell with *Islander*, came closest. He died in Cape Town just months
before completing three circumnavigations alone with the same boat. We
met Tom in Mauritius on our first voyage, when he was preparing for his
last passage. John Sowden's third voyage was completed in Martinique,

and if he were not so laid-back and modest, the whole world would know about him. Instead, after a long passage from Durban, with only one stop in Saint Helena and a spell of being becalmed for two weeks at the equator, he arrived quietly at Fort-de-France and anchored in the middle of the bay, 1,000 yards from the other boats. It was a pleasure to be the first to congratulate him, and he asked to buy a copy of our first book. We felt privileged to be able to give him one. Ironically, John may be able to use it to remember his voyages in which he visited many of the same ports, because he never took any photographs. He is one of the few circumnavigators not writing a book. When I asked him if he planned to make a fourth voyage, he said, "Not a chance!"

In Martinique, fruit was so expensive that we decided to sail to Dominica to get our own. There we traded extra tins of chicken, Danish ham, and beverage drink mixes for huge stalks of bananas and 200 grapefruit. On our first world voyage, we had done the same in exchange for rocks. I had wanted more weight because once our food was gone, we lost that ballast, and this was the cheapest and easiest way to replace it. Once we got back to Maine, we threw the rocks overboard and replaced them with lead.

From Dominica, we proceeded on to Antigua, only 150 miles away, and arrived on April 3. A low island that has been developed for tourism, Antigua boasts 365 beaches, one for every day of the year. Millions of dollars worth of yachts were anchored in English Harbour, where there is a port fee for everything. Water costs 20 cents a gallon, and groceries and diesel are also expensive, so we decided to sail over to St. Thomas in the U.S. Virgin Islands to resupply. Fortunately, I was able to sell some spare gear for $800.

On the way to St. Thomas, we stopped for a day at Nevis, where Alexander Hamilton was born. His former home now is a museum. There we met a Peace Corps couple from New Hampshire, who invited us to lunch.

St. Thomas is American but with a style of its own. A fantastic grocery store provided us with everything we needed, and diesel fuel was $2 less per gallon than in Antigua. On the main waterfront street were all the American fast-food restaurants, and five tourist ships arrived daily. The *Norway* and the *Queen Elizabeth II*, world's largest ocean liners, were both there, and everything was bustling. There were hundreds of duty-free shops. The Baskin-Robbins ice cream parlor was a mecca for Tommy and Lisa, and Arby's Roast Beef (the only Arby's I have ever seen with a bar) had happy hour every afternoon and was well patronized by everyone on board. There were also hundreds of duty-free shops.

Appledore *at Bermuda.*

Heinz Stucke, world traveling bicyclist.

Homeward Bound

On April 15, we departed St. Thomas for Bermuda. The northeast tradewinds were nonexistent and we motored northward with a light southerly breeze. For three days, we had to use the engine. Halfway to Bermuda, we began to get cooler weather and northwest winds. This required driving *Appledore* hard into the swell, but eventually we arrived in Bermuda. It was April 22. How good it felt to be back. One-and-a-half years earlier, we had departed from Bermuda, bound around the world. This is one of our favorite islands. We tied up behind *American Promise*, the boat that Dodge Morgan sailed around the world in only five months. *Appledore* made a remarkable contrast to his high-tech vessel.

In Bermuda, we painted all the exterior surfaces of *Appledore* so we would be ready for taking out passengers the weekend after we returned to Boothbay Harbor. We gave ourselves 10 days to make Boothbay Harbor, figuring that would give us three extra days, because we had done the passage twice before in seven days. However, this passage would be different.

We left Bermuda on May 1 and started tacking into light northwest headwinds. I knew a cold front was coming off the East Coast, and we would have to put up with its effects in two days. I did not look forward to it. By the time we were 300 miles north of Bermuda, we were in a full gale. To make matters worse, we were right in the middle of the Gulf Stream. If the wind had been from the east, we would have had to run south and get out of the current, because the seas that make up when the wind opposes the current are extremely dangerous. They are virtually walls of destruction.

We did have winds of 50 knots, and it was uncomfortable but not serious. The winds came from the west, with the current. Eventually the wind let up and we got out of the Gulf Stream, only to get into another

Sailing into Boothbay Harbor, Maine. Peter E. Randall photo.

gale. This time, the wind was from the southwest, a fair breeze, and we
took advantage of it to make the best possible time.

A hundred miles southeast of Cape Cod, we finally found some
smooth water, though it was extremely cold — 38° at night. However, the
smell and look of the sea indicated we were back in New England waters.
We were also within range of the NOAA weather broadcast on the VHF
radio, so we knew exactly what to expect in the next 24 hours. Incredibly,
another gale was forecast, but in 24 hours, we would be past Cape Cod
and off Cape Ann. The gale was predicted for Georges Bank.

By noon on Thursday, May 8, we were sailing off the Isles of Shoals
when the wind came against us. We anchored behind Appledore Island
and all took pictures of Doris's father's former house. The next day, we
sat out a northeast gale at anchor. It was nice to have missed that one. On
Saturday morning, we got underway for Boothbay Harbor with a light
northerly wind. This would be the last time we hoisted the sails together,
and the voyage was practically over. Our pet hamster had survived the
entire voyage. It was a calm passage down the coast. It was hard to
imagine that we had just spent 18 months sailing around the world. We
reflected a bit on all the ports of call we had made. They seemed such a
long time ago. During the voyage, we had had a lot of time to relax and
set new goals, and now we were anxious to get on with them. The clock
of life was ticking.

The Smith family in Boothbay Harbor after completing their second world voyage. Boutilier photo.

Coming home on Mother's Day, May 11, was an exciting finale to our adventure. At dawn, we were just 12 miles outside Boothbay Harbor, and as the sky brightened, I could see the Maine coast ahead. At 45° farenheit, the air was cool and invigorating, which I thoroughly enjoyed. I am not too keen on the tropics, preferring the changing New England seasons. It can be cold enough for a frost in the morning yet in the seventies by noon, and this kind of contrast makes for an interesting day. In the South Pacific, if the temperature changed that drastically, the whole population would perish, along with all the vegetation.

My brother Steve had made arrangements with U.S. Customs to come out at noon for clearance. Once that was taken care of, we pointed the bow toward the harbor. The passenger ship *Argo*, with Captain Pete Ripley on board, came out to welcome us home, and there were many more well-wishers in small boats, with the Coast Guard escorting us directing the spray from fire hoses in the air.. Along the shore, people waved to us. It was a great welcome. This was an old-fashioned homecoming, much as in the days when the icebreaker *Eastwind* returned from Antarctica. Only by being away for a year and a half without seeing close friends does one ever experience something like this. I wonder how the old whaling ship crews felt after returning from a four-year voyage.

We sailed into the harbor with full sail set and drawing. I knew there would be a lot of happy mothers waiting ashore, but the welcome was much bigger than I could have imagined. People had even come from as far away as Oregon and South Africa. The biggest and most thrilling event was receiving the key to the town of Boothbay Harbor from the town manager, Malcolm Hunter. For an ordinary person like myself, it was a great honor and privilege. I am sure the rest of the crew felt the same way. No one could have thought of a kinder, more appreciated gesture.

We were also grateful to all the others who helped with the reception that followed. The Chamber of Commerce, friends, and relatives put much thought and work into making our homecoming memorable. We had been through a lot of difficulties and hardships, but, thank God, we had made it home safe and sound. *Appledore* had served us well, and I was particularly happy to see 80-year-old Bud McIntosh on the dock watching his schooner come home.

TIME AND DISTANCE TABLE

Ports of call:	Distance:	Arrival:	Departure:
Boothbay Harbor, Maine			Nov. 5, 1984
St. Georges, Bermuda	740	Nov. 12, 1984	Nov. 17, 1984
Fortaleza, Brazil	2725	Dec. 13, 1984	Dec. 15, 1984
Recife, Brazil	440	Dec. 19, 1984	Dec. 27, 1984
Rio de Janeiro, Brazil	920	Jan. 5, 1985	Jan. 16, 1985
Mar Del Plata, Argentina	1200	Jan. 26, 1985	Jan. 28, 1985
Punta Arenas, Chile	1185	Feb. 7, 1985	Feb. 17, 1985
Playa Parda, Strait of Magellan	125	Feb. 19, 1985	Feb. 24, 1985
Angosto Cove, Strait of Magellan	30	Feb. 24, 1985	Feb. 25, 1985
Bahia Fortun, Patagonia, Chile	65	Feb. 25, 1985	Feb. 26, 1985
Dacres Islands, Chile	115	Feb. 28, 1985	March 1, 1985
Port Eden, Chile	85	March 6, 1985	March 7, 1985
Seno Iceberg, Chile	40	March 7, 1985	March 8, 1985
Fleurisis Cove, Chile	65	March 9, 1985	March 10, 1985
Puerto Montt, Chile	425	March 14, 1985	March 24, 1985
Robinson Crusoe Island, Chile	550	March 29, 1985	March 30, 1985
Easter Island, Chile	1700	April 15, 1985	April 17, 1985
Pitcairn Island	1250	April 28, 1985	April 30, 1985
Tahiti, French Polynesia	1200	May 10, 1985	May 22, 1985
Moorea, French Polynesia	16	May 22, 1985	May 27, 1985
Tahiti, French Polynesia	16	May 27, 1985	June 3, 1985
American Samoa	1200	June 15, 1985	June 19, 1985
Suva, Fiji	720	June 25, 1985	July 1, 1985
Port Vila, Vanuatu	600	July 5, 1985	July 8, 1985
Port Moresby, New Guinea	1300	July 18, 1985	July 22, 1985
Rennel Island, Torres Straits	280	July 23, 1985	July 24, 1985
Darwin, Australia	720	July 30, 1985	Aug. 12, 1985
Bali, Indonesia	950	Aug. 21, 1985	Aug. 31, 1985
Christmas Island, Indian Ocean	580	Sept. 5, 1985	Sept. 7, 1985
Cocos Islands	550	Sept. 10, 1985	Sept. 12, 1985
Rodrigues Island	2000	Sept. 25, 1985	Sept. 28, 1985
Port Louis, Mauritius	380	Oct. 1, 1985	Oct. 9, 1985
Reunion Island	132	Oct. 10, 1985	Oct. 17, 1985
Durban, South Africa	1500	Oct. 27, 1985	Dec. 12, 1985
East London, South Africa	240	Dec. 13, 1985	Dec.. 15, 1985
Mussel Bay, South Africa	310	Dec. 17, 1985	Dec. 19, 1985
Cape Town, South Africa	190	Dec. 21, 1985	Jan. 25, 1986
St. Helena, Atlantic Ocean	1700	Feb. 7, 1986	Feb. 10, 1986
Ascension Island	700	Feb. 18, 1986	Feb. 19, 1986
Barbado, Caribbean	2986	March 12, 1986	March 20, 1986
Martinique	131	March 21, 1986	April 1, 1986
Dominica	45	April 2, 1986	April 3, 1986
English Harbor, Antigua	110	April 4, 1986	April 7, 1986
Nevis	50	April 8, 1986	April 8, 1986
St. Thomas, U.S. Virgin Islands	155	April 10, 1986	April 15, 1986
Bermuda	830	April 22, 1986	May 1, 1986
Boothbay Harbor, Maine	740	May 11, 1986	

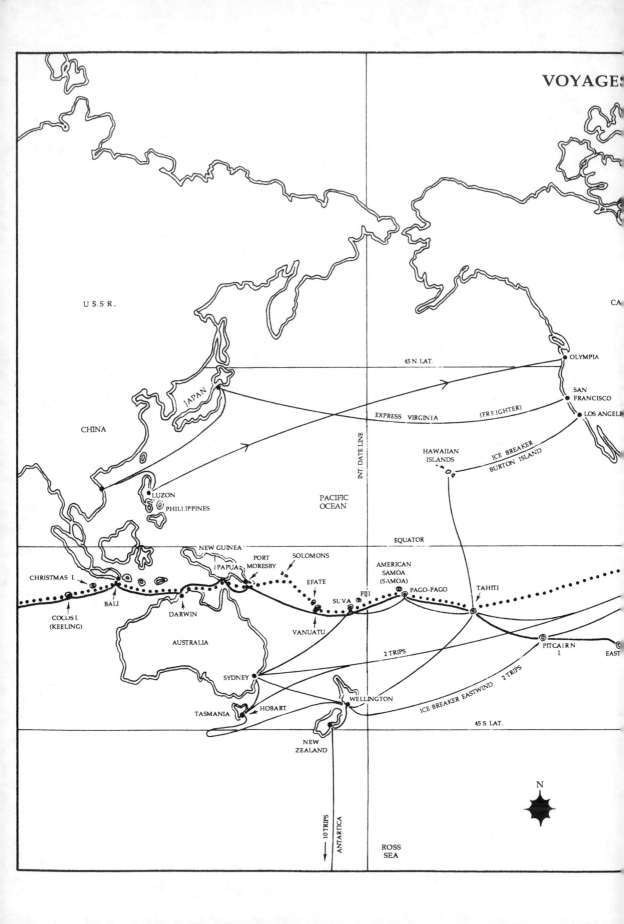

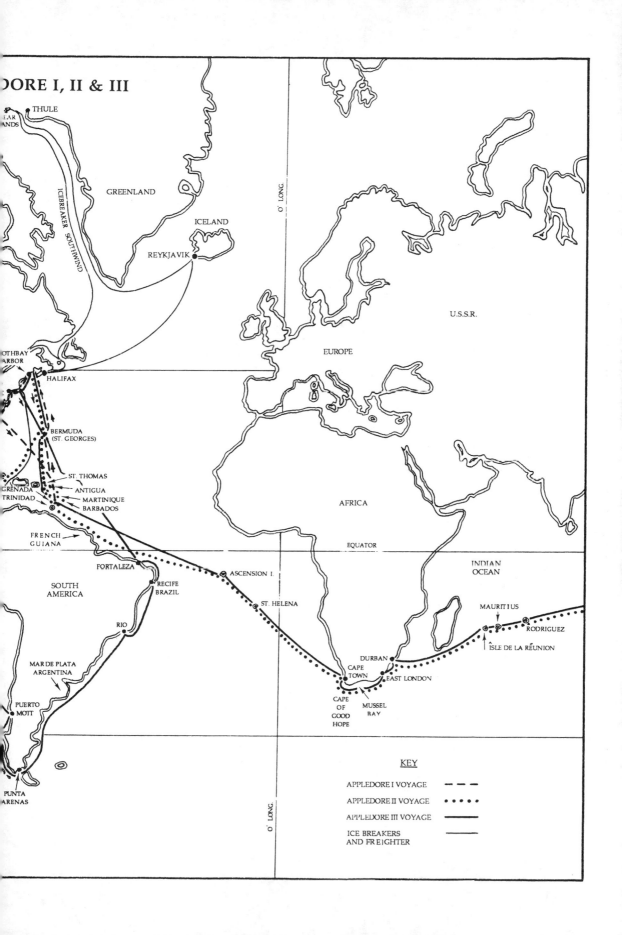

DORE I, II & III

THULE

EAR ANDS

GREENLAND

ICELAND

REYKJAVIK

ICEBREAKER SOUTHWIND

O' LONG.

U.S.S.R.

EUROPE

OTHBAY ARBOR

HALIFAX

BERMUDA
(ST. GEORGES)

ST. THOMAS

GRENADA — ANTIGUA
TRINIDAD — MARTINIQUE
BARBADOS

AFRICA

FRENCH
GUIANA

EQUATOR

FORTALEZA

INDIAN
OCEAN

RECIFE
BRAZIL

SOUTH
AMERICA

ASCENSION I.

ST. HELENA

MAURITIUS

RIO

RODRIGUEZ

ISLE DE LA RÉUNION

MAR DE PLATA
ARGENTINA

DURBAN

CAPE
TOWN

EAST LONDON

PUERTO
MOTT

CAPE
OF
GOOD
HOPE

MUSSEL
BAY

PUNTA
ARENAS

O' LONG.

KEY

APPLEDORE I VOYAGE — — —

APPLEDORE II VOYAGE • • • • •

APPLEDORE III VOYAGE —————

ICE BREAKERS
AND FREIGHTER ————